Languages and Social Cohesion

A critical and systematic review of existing research located at the cross-roads of sociology, social psychology and applied linguistics, *Languages and Social Cohesion* offers valuable insights for social contexts in which decision makers and researchers grapple with questions of social cohesion in the presence of linguistic diversity.

Based on a thematic analysis of 285 studies from 50 countries (references available), this book emphasises the crucial role languages play in understanding social cohesion and provides a framework of perspectives to aid exploration of these complex interlinkages. Through interpreting the literature, the authors establishe language repertoires as tools that facilitate social networks and access to resources. Furthermore, language norms and allegiances can subjectively shape the way groups use their language resources, which can result in social inclusion, exclusion and mediation between language groups.

Education in particular is highlighted as a policy tool that implements linguistic decisions and norms, and steers status, hierarchies and distribution of languages in society. The theory-informed and accessible tools featured can be used to guide and inform further research, workshops or projects that investigate social cohesion and languages. This book is relevant to diverse and intersecting spheres of influence, such as groups, communities, institutions and authorities at local, regional, national and international levels.

Gabriela Meier is Senior Lecturer in Language Education in the Graduate School of Education of the College for Social Sciences and International Studies at the University of Exeter, UK. She has worked as a researcher, language teacher educator and supervisor of doctoral projects at the universities of Bath and Exeter (UK). She has published in English, German and French in fields related to language education and social cohesion. Recent publications include *Multilingual Socialisation in Education* (2018) and *The Multilingual Turn as a Critical Movement in Education* (2017).

Simone Smala is Senior Lecturer in Education in the School of Education in the Faculty of Humanities, Arts and Social Sciences at the University of Queensland, Australia. Her research on languages and cultural capital is set in Content and Language Integrated Learning (CLIL) and Bilingual Education programmes, with a focus on curriculum choices and language learning strategies. She publishes in English and German.

Routledge Advances in Sociology

For more information about this series, please visit: www.routledge.com/Routledge-Advances-in-Sociology/book-series/SE0511

Languages and Social Cohesion

A Transdisciplinary Literature Review

Gabriela Meier and Simone Smala

Routledge
Taylor & Francis Group

LONDON AND NEW YORK

First published 2022
by Routledge
2 Park Square, Milton Park, Abingdon, Oxon OX14 4RN

and by Routledge
605 Third Avenue, New York, NY 10158

Routledge is an imprint of the Taylor & Francis Group, an informa business

British Library Cataloguing-in-Publication Data
A catalogue record for this book is available from the British Library

Library of Congress Cataloging-in-Publication Data
Names: Meier, Gabriela, 1965– author. | Smala, Simone, author.
Title: Languages and social cohesion : a transdisciplinary
literature review / Gabriela Meier and Simone Smala.
Description: Abingdon, Oxon ; New York, NY : Routledge, 2021. |
Series: Routledge advances in sociology |
Includes bibliographical references and index.
Identifiers: LCCN 2021014132 (print) | LCCN 2021014133 (ebook) |
ISBN 9780367637200 (hbk) | ISBN 9780367638146 (pbk) |
ISBN 9781003120384 (ebk)
Subjects: LCSH: Social psychology. | Social psychology
and literature. | Linguistics.
Classification: LCC HM1033 .M437 2021 (print) |
LCC HM1033 (ebook) | DDC 808.8/0353–dc23
LC record available at https://lccn.loc.gov/2021014132
LC ebook record available at https://lccn.loc.gov/2021014133

ISBN: 978-0-367-63720-0 (hbk)
ISBN: 978-0-367-63814-6 (pbk)
ISBN: 978-1-003-12038-4 (ebk)

DOI: 10.4324/9781003120384

Typeset in Times New Roman
by Newgen Publishing UK

Contents

Figures

Tables

Acknowledgements

Many people have contributed to this book. First of all we thank the University of Exeter (UK) and the University of Queensland (Australia) who supported this project financially. We thank all the wonderful colleagues globally whose research inspired this book. It is their work, located at the crossroads where languages and social cohesion research intersect, which enabled us to conduct this transdisciplinary literature review. Members of the research team were instrumental to this project, and we could not have produced this book without them. Helen Lawson, our research fellow at the University of Exeter, contributed substantially to the development of our research methodology. In particular she developed our systematic article searches and screening, as described in Chapter 3. Ralph Openshaw, our volunteer research assistant, supported the project by engaging with analysis, critical comments, formatting, proofreading and much more. Huong Nguyen, our research assistant at the University of Queensland, helped develop the EndNote Library that is now available for download (Meier, Smala & Lawson, 2021). Furthermore, we extend our thanks to our esteemed and generous colleagues, including Prof. Deborah Myhill and Prof. Dongbo Zhang (University of Exeter), as well as Prof. Emeritus Adil Khan (University of Queensland), who commented on earlier versions of this book, engaging critically with our work at different points in the project. We also thank the anonymous Routledge peer reviewers who commented on our book proposal, further helping us to sharpen our analysis and thinking. Our families, friends and colleagues deserve thanks for their patience and encouragement during the life of this project (2018–2021). Lastly, we are grateful to the Routledge Focus Series editorial team, especially Emily Briggs and Lakshita Joshi who believed in and supported this project on its way to publication.

Thank you, danke, merci, gracias, cảm ơn, 谢谢, ধন্যবাদ, धन्यवाद ...!

1 Introduction

Researching languages and social cohesion

Language is crucial for human communication, collaboration, the relationships we build and the way we understand our place in the world. In a world increasingly influenced by globalisation, including migration of people and the Internet, linguistic diversity is, or is becoming, a reality in many people's lives. In situations where different languages and language groups meet, social cohesion is sometimes seen as a challenge. In contrast, language educators tend to emphasise the value of language competences as a source of social cohesion. We thus embarked on a journey to examine the link between languages and social cohesion in situations where various languages and language varieties come into contact with one another, which resulted in this book.

The fact that languages can lead to both conflict and peaceful communication (Vetter, 2015) served as a starting point for this book. While language conflict is an established strand in the field of sociology of language, the specific link between languages and social cohesion has not been researched widely. In order to establish what we know about this link between languages and social cohesion, we embarked on a systematic literature review. Our overarching aim was therefore to investigate in which ways research literature has associated languages with social cohesion, both as an enabler and as a barrier. As will be seen in this book, languages can be used to unite, divide or mediate within and between language groups in complex, dynamic and subtle ways.

The way we learn, use and organise languages in specific social contexts and societies is typically examined from various perspectives and disciplines, above all within the field of wider applied linguistics, but also in social psychology and sociology. We have therefore taken a transdisciplinary approach to conducting our literature review, as this "brings information from separate disciplines together so that it can be useful knowledge that allows us to act wisely" (Montuori, 2013, p. 47). This approach allowed us to view the link between languages

DOI: 10.4324/9781003120384-1

and social cohesion in their complexity rather than from a single perspective. By looking at languages and social cohesion largely at group level, our work complements the wider literature on language identity, language and intercultural competence (e.g. Norton & Toohey, 2011; Pavlenko & Norton, 2007; Byram, Nichols & Stevens, 2001), as well as literature on linguistic capital and similar concepts that tend to look at language use and social participation at an individual level (Gerhards, 2014; May, 2014; de Swaan, 2001; Bourdieu, 1991). Furthermore, it complements research on language policy and planning (Ricento, 2014; May & Hornberger, 2008; Wright, 2004), language mediation (Corbett, 2020; González-Davies, 2020; Council of Europe, 2018) and particularly research on language conflict (Darquennes, 2015; Vetter, 2015).

Context of this book

We are writing this book at a particular time in history, and it is against this background that we developed our interest in the relationships between languages and social cohesion. We look on with increasing concern as the world faces ever greater challenges. We are acutely aware of the increasingly globalised relationships between phenomena of our times and concur that they are "deeply connected, and our understanding, appreciation, and responses should be shaped accordingly" (Brown, 2018, p. 1).

We are concerned that divided societies may be vulnerable and ill-equipped to deal with the enormous global challenges we face in the coming decades. That said, socially cohesive societies are seen as more resilient and able to cope with challenges than divided societies (UNDP, 2020, p. 12), and indeed social cohesion is associated with problem-solving through social networks connecting different groups (Schiefer & van der Noll, 2017; Putnam, 2000). We assume it is for this reason that the United Nations continues to focus on social cohesion and inclusion, as an important aspect of its Sustainable Development Goals (United Nations, 2015) where "No One Left Behind" is the core theme, albeit with no mention of languages. A more recent UN document, entitled *Strengthening social cohesion: Conceptual framing and programming implications*, also reinforces the importance of social cohesion (UNDP, 2020). This document does touch on languages – as one factor among many – in respect to participation, human-rights agendas and non-discrimination.

As we will show in this book, languages are interconnected with social cohesion in many nuanced and complex ways, and we feel social cohesion projects, policy and research that do not take the language factor into consideration may be overlooking a substantive influence on the operation of societies. In the following, we further describe our motivation to write this book, define key concepts we use and outline the scope, aims and intended readership of this book.

Key definitions

Research into languages as a societal phenomenon suggests that we need a closer examination of the role languages play as an enabling or disrupting force in societies (Riera-Gil, 2019; Ricento, 2014; Wodak, 2007) and as a resource in itself (Ruiz, 2010). Literature from different fields postulates that often neither the uniting *nor* the divisive potential of languages are sufficiently considered in social policy conceptualisations or political theory (Osler & Lybaek, 2014; Ricento, 2014). Furthermore, social cohesion is sometimes an assumed consequence of language education policies, such as the Common European Framework of Reference for Languages (Council of Europe, 2001) or certain language teaching methods (see, for example, Coyle, Hood & Marsh, 2010 in their book *CLIL* or *Content and Language Integrated Learning*), without reference to the nature of that connection.

At the outset of our project, we defined languages and social cohesion as *separate* concepts to gain some clarity of the concepts. While this was our starting point, the literature review presented in the following chapters lays open the complex, nuanced and unpredictable ways languages and social cohesion are intertwined.

Social cohesion: In research and policy documents, the term *social cohesion* is often used synonymously with social integration, community cohesion, social inclusion or social capital. Social cohesion is a concern of social psychologists and sociologists alike, and has been described as ambiguous, complex and multidimensional (Kearns & Forrest, 2000). Taking the lead from some recent literature reviews on social cohesion (Schiefer & van der Noll, 2017; Chan, To & Chan, 2006) and relevant articles looking at languages and social cohesion (Jenson, 2019; Stolle, 2013; Kearns & Forrest, 2000), we agreed on a number of dimensions, such as 'social networks and associated resources', 'a sense of belonging to groups' and 'shared norms and values'. These dimensions are included in established definitions of social cohesion, as proposed by key sociologists (see, for example, Field, 2003; Lin, 2001; Putnam, 2000; Coleman, 1988; Bourdieu, 1986; Granovetter, 1983, 1973), and will be explained further in Chapter 2.

Languages: Language is also hard to define, as it is viewed differently by different scholars. Some view it as a stable and formalised linguistic structure or a system that can be studied, while others view it as a means of identification and/or social practice (Norton & McKinney, 2011). Furthermore, languages have been conceptualised as political constructs and as sites of struggle (Sarroub & Quadros, 2014) which interlink with sociopolitical decisions and discourses (Canagarajah, 2013). Languages and varieties are also associated with identification (Norton & McKinney, 2011), as people use languages and language varieties to index belonging to certain linguistic groups (Blommaert, 2010). In popular and academic discourses, languages are often labelled, for instance as *first* or *second*, as *modern* or *heritage*, or as *official* or *migrant* languages, thus implying an order by acquisition, quality or status associated with languages, which potentially stereotypes languages and their users (see, for example, Cruickshank, 2014, who made this point). Using these categories is, however, difficult to avoid in projects like ours. While being aware of the risks, we use such labels in this book, since they can make visible possible assumptions that people have about languages, and about groups who are using these languages. This anticipates a golden thread leading through this book, namely that languages are not only of instrumental, communicative and practical value, but also hold a symbolic and subjective value in societies, which is neither stable nor neutral (Ricento, 2014).

Scope and aims

In this book, we structure, critically analyse and discuss a body of 285 peer-reviewed articles, published between 1992 and 2017, in the light of wider literature, with the aim to establish any links between languages and social cohesion. This work enabled us to offer accessible and user-friendly tools designed to inspire discussion about the interconnecting dimensions of languages and social cohesion in a given context. Our work thus resulted in thematically sorted list of references, a transdisciplinary language and social cohesion framework, and a set of respective questions, as summarised in Chapter 5. This framework of relevant perspectives is underpinned by our analysis in Chapter 4 and offers an understanding of the language–social cohesion interlinkages. These tools can be used as an exploratory guide by readers involved in social contexts where languages and social cohesion might emerge as a topic of concern. It is important to note that this book cannot offer recipes or generalisable explanations of cause and effect; instead we will describe how relevant concepts interconnect in many different social contexts, indicating *possibilities* of cause and effect between languages and social cohesion.

Authors and potential biases

This book has been written by authors currently residing in the UK and Australia. However, its relevance is global. Indeed, the research included in our review stems from 50 countries or regions, including Europe, Asia, Australia and Oceania, Africa, and North and South America, featuring research with language groups of very diverse origins. Our study included research from multilingual nations and from the developing world (e.g. India, Sri Lanka, Bangladesh, Botswana, South Africa, Ghana, Mexico, Bolivia), but we assume that unequal access to English-language publishing and systemic academic bias means that highly multilingual countries such as India, Nigeria, Tanzania, and Vanuatu may not be adequately represented in our study.

While we aim to take an objective stance in this book to describe different world views, our own linguistic repertoires, as well as social, professional and migratory experiences, alongside our engagement with research, have informed ours. Thus, we have developed a strong leaning towards transculturalism, as described by Stolle (2013), insofar as we welcome and accept linguistic diversity as a reality, but we understand that not everyone shares this view. Indeed, tensions can arise between different views of how languages should be organised in a society – such subjective views and ideas will resurface in the following chapters, as these are important factors that influence how languages and social cohesion interlink. On the basis of these observations, we set ourselves two objectives. The first was to develop an evidence-informed and transdisciplinary understanding of the relationships between languages and social cohesion, guided by the following research question: *In what way are languages associated with social cohesion in academic articles?* The second objective was to structure and illustrate evidence located in the area where multiple disciplines overlap, and make this accessible for a wide audience of stakeholders and practitioners, as well as academic researchers, as described in the next section.

Intended readership

This book is envisaged for readers who may have specific contexts in mind, where hierarchies, tensions and conflicts between language communities might exist or be suspected, and where an interlinked language and social cohesion lens, such as the one we propose, may offer a theory-informed and accessible way of exploring the powers that may be at play in such situations, so that appropriate and context-sensitive action can follow. In Chapter 5, we provide a transdisciplinary framework of what we learnt from the literature and offer questions (see Table 5.1) for stakeholders as practical starting points to reflect on ways in which languages and social cohesion may be connected in their contexts or spheres of life. The questions aim to sharpen awareness of the possibilities, challenges and risks. Beyond this book, we make available a thematically structured and downloadable bibliography in the form of an EndNote Library (Meier, Smala & Lawson, 2021, https://data.mendeley.com/datasets/ydtms99mjm/3), which can serve as a source of information for policymakers, researchers and practitioners. The transdisciplinary framework, questions and EndNote Library are tools applicable in a host of contexts where the details of languages and social cohesion need to be explored. Such contexts may include:

- local community organisations (e.g. sport, youth, charity and religious groups and clubs);
- social and health sectors (e.g. hospitals, residential homes, care sector);
- companies (e.g. retail, wholesale, service sector, production, development and innovation sites);
- educational institutions (e.g. schools, colleges, universities, adult education, life-long learning);
- government agencies or ministries (e.g. councils, education ministries, police, domestic and international policy units);
- non-governmental international organisations (e.g. NGOs and supranational bodies working in development, peace, social and ecological sustainability);
- research contexts (e.g. applied linguistics, government studies, international relations, development studies, different linguistic and educational fields, sociology, social psychology or political science).

Chapter outlines

Chapter 1 introduces the rationale and disciplinary lenses, context, concepts and scope, as well as intended readership of our book, and offers an overview of the content.

Chapter 2 establishes our conceptual categories on languages and social cohesion at the crossroads where disciplinary angles overlap. On the basis of a transdisciplinary scoping review of literature, we define relevant terms and concepts we used for our systematic literature search and describe the gap in research as well as the lack of practical guidance for decision makers. This review shows similarities and discrepancies between the perspectives, and defines concepts that influenced research design, analysis and interpretation of findings. This chapter provides the reasons and broad structural approaches that guided our systematic literature review of languages and social cohesion.

Chapter 3 describes and justifies the rigorous approaches we adopted to identify and thematically analyse relevant peer-reviewed articles published between 1992 and 2017, which help answer our research question. It describes how we screened and assessed the 16,625 articles initially returned by our search for eligibility, following the PRISMA protocol (Moher, Liberati, Tetzlaff, Altman & the PRISMA group, 2009), and the exclusion and inclusion processes. We describe how we arrived at the body of 285 articles we included and offer a first broad descriptive analysis, including information on research methods. The thematic analysis approach we used is also outlined and illustrated. Thus, it describes the development of our data set, its characteristics and how we analysed it to develop our themes.

Chapter 4 presents the results of our analysis under five main themes and 14 related sub-themes. These themes structure the findings and illustrate these with examples from multiple contexts. The themes comprise: (A) social networks and resources potentially enabled through languages; (B) norms, values and attitudes related to languages and language groups; (C) feelings of group belonging informed by languages; (D) manifestations of societal behaviour in which languages play a role; and (E) language planning or decision making and its potential consequences for social cohesion. These themes are compared, and complemented with insights from Chapter 2 to establish, discuss and interpret the diverse links that have been made in the literature we analysed between languages and social cohesion.

Chapter 5 makes visible our unique contribution to knowledge, by drawing together all strands of our literature review, discussions and interpretations, and restructures the extant literature established in Chapters 2 and 4 into a new transdisciplinary framework featuring six interlinked perspectives from which the topic under scrutiny can be approached and examined. This is accompanied by theory-informed and accessible questions that are offered to readers wishing to explore languages and social cohesion in specific sociopolitical contexts beyond this book.

2 Languages and social cohesion

Key concepts and disciplinary overlaps

This chapter draws on a range of academic fields to map and explore key concepts that underpin our project. This preliminary review of literature, which Dijkers (2015) might consider a scoping review, establishes research insights and theoretical concepts, as well as the link between languages and social cohesion, from different disciplinary perspectives. These insights are typically understood as originating from separate fields of study, each with their own university departments, journals and spheres of application.

Specifically, this chapter first maps the relevant fields, before it defines the concepts which informed our systematic literature search and analysis, as described in Chapter 3. Thus, it offers initial insights into the links between key concepts, which are then expanded and discussed in Chapter 4, which is based on the body of literature we identified through our systematic literature search. We also offer a first insight into the way disciplines we draw on overlap or diverge, with the view to invite ongoing conversations in a transdisciplinary way. In the following, we will first turn to literature from the wide field of applied linguistics to establish how language can be understood for the purpose of our project. We then turn to literature on social cohesion and related fields.

Conceptualisation of languages and links to social cohesion

Applied linguistics, the definition of which is arguably multidisciplinary, ambiguous and contested, is said to draw on sociology, psychology, anthropology, information theory and linguistics (Hejwowski, 2018). Cook (2003) specifies that applied linguistics comprises language education (first, additional; second, foreign language education, speech impairments, language testing); language used in work and law (workplace communication, language planning, forensic linguistics) and language information and effect (literary stylistics, critical

DOI: 10.4324/9781003120384-2

discourse analysis, translation and interpretation, information design, lexicography). To this list, we add language policy and planning (Goundar, 2017), as well as sociolinguistics and sociology of language (Darquennes, 2015). There is a common denominator noticeable within all these sub-areas of applied linguistics, namely that the field is inter-disciplinary and studies "language problems that are relevant to the everyday lives of individuals, groups of individuals, or entire societies and cultures" (Berns & Matsuda, 2006, p. 394). Such understandings go back to Brumfit's much-cited definition, which describes applied linguistics as "the theoretical and empirical investigation of real-world problems in which language is a central issue" (1995, p. 27). For the purpose of this book, we draw on the arguably distinct disciplines that are covered under this broader umbrella field of applied linguistics, including sociolinguistics, sociology of language, language policy and planning, and language education.

We selected these disciplines as they seek to understand the connection between languages and social cohesion, among other concerns. *Sociolinguistics* is concerned with the study of how societies affect language: more precisely how "the history of social relations among populations, including economic, political and demographic factors" influences the use of language(s) and language varieties (Sankoff, 2001, p. 3). The related field of *sociology of language* is interested in how language affects society (Darquennes, 2015; Vetter, 2015). *Language policy and planning* is a research field that is concerned with how languages are organised in a given society, including in the public sphere, media and education (Ricento, 2014; Wright, 2004). *Language education* seen from this perspective can therefore overlap with all the disciplines above. Thus, we draw on literature from these disciplines to develop a defin-ition of language and how this may relate to social cohesion.

Defining language

Language has been conceptualised differently over time and in different fields. It has been conceptualised as a fixed code or system (de Saussure, 1966), as an instrument for communication (Halliday, 1985), as a dynamic tool for social action (Atkinson, 2011) and for mediation (Council of Europe, 2018; Lantolf, 2011) as well as a tool for identification (Norton & McKinney, 2011) that occurs in zones of contact between language groups (Vetter, 2015). In addition, language has been defined through the perspective of multilingualism over the last 30–40 years, in response to increased awareness of languages in societies. This has been termed the multilingual turn (Conteh & Meier, 2014; May, 2014). Intertwined with this, critical perspectives have been developed looking at languages and their political, social and ideological dimensions (Blommaert, 2006; Pennycook, 2001; Skutnabb-Kangas, 1981). Included in these perspectives are understandings of language as an instrumental tool, as a multilingual resource, as an expression of allegiance and as a political-ideological construct, as well as the organisation of all these in society. We will focus on these aspects as relevant for our project.

Instrumental view of language

First, we turn to Blommaert (2006) and Ricento (2014), representatives of sociolinguistics and language policy and planning respectively, who both make a similar point. Blommaert argues that the Saussurean notion of language as a "transparent, structured, and finite system", or as an artefact or object that a person "can obtain, possess, manufacture and improve", is the most widely adopted conceptualisation of language in scientific as well as in popular circles (2006, p. 511). In this view, language is considered to be neutral, and belonging to a certain "language community" of native speakers, which suggests allegiance with an imagined homogenous, bounded and stable group (Blommaert, 2006, p. 511). This notion takes for granted that a common language enables successful transmission of knowledge between people. While no one refutes this potential, "the actual contexts of its acquisition, transmission, and use in daily life" (Ricento, 2014, p. 352) are frequently not considered in scholarly works in many fields, as Ricento argues in his article, "Thinking about language: what political theorists need to know about language in the real world". He describes, for example, political theorists as "generally non-experts in the language sciences" who tend to understand language in a simplistic way based on its "instrumental and symbolic value" (2014, p. 351). This instrumental view typically treats a standardised version of a given language as the only version, ignoring "sociolinguistic differences" such as language varieties, dialects and accents that occur within a language (Blommaert, 2006, 351). We strongly embrace the notion, based in descriptive linguistics, that there are arguably no linguistic criteria to distinguish languages and dialects, and that standard languages are not linguistically superior to dialect versions (see also NicCraith, 2000). Blommaert (2006) reminds us that a standard language is just one variety among many other social and regional language varieties, and constitutes the variety that has become accepted as self-evident and as the norm. From this point of view, language is not neutral, as we need to consider "inequalities which often result for persons who [...] may be perceived to be members of named ethnolinguistic minority communities which may further marginalize their social status" (Ricento, 2014, p. 365). These views are critical starting points for an understanding of social cohesion and languages, and informed our theoretical approach towards developing our systematic literature review project. Having questioned the arguably monolithic understanding of what languages are, we now interrogate languages as part of our social world.

Language repertoire as a social resource

Focusing on languages as spoken and used in many contexts around us, Blommaert (2006) makes an important distinction between *communicative linguistic repertoires* and *communicative practices*, which illustrates the difference between language potential and language uses in real-life situations. For particular forms of communicative practice (Blommaert uses the example of exchanging gossip), specific linguistic resources or repertoires have to be activated (e.g. the use of a regional accent). Sharing an accent, or using differing language varieties, can therefore denote affiliations, but also affect negotiations of social positioning (e.g. who can initiate a conversation, how intimacy is signalled, and so on). Languages have therefore been theorised as part of a person's multiple communicative resources as part of a linguistic repertoire (Blommaert, 2006). This can include, for instance, an informal regional accent for conversations with local friends, as well as other language varieties that are used for more formal, less intimate communication such as for work or study, depending on prevalent local language norms. Added to this are foreign or other languages that again are activated in specific social situations. Aligning with this understanding of languages and their varieties as a social resource for communicative practices in varied contexts, the influential and widely cited Common European Framework of Reference for Languages, or CEFR for short (Council of Europe, 2001), proposes languages to mean a person's *language repertoire*. Such a repertoire encapsulates all written and spoken forms of languages a person might use in society, as well as forms of language people might learn inside and outside of educational environments, including language varieties, dialects, signed languages and partial languages (Busch, 2012). This view of languages is based on the idea of plurilingualism (Council of Europe, 2001, 2018), which assumes that "individuals develop competences in a number of languages [and language varieties], from desire or necessity, in order to meet the need to communicate with others" (Coste, Moore & Zarate, 2009).

Being able to use certain forms and varieties of language has been described by Bourdieu (1991), a renowned sociologist, as linguistic capital, a form of cultural capital that people can use to access high-level institutions like schools and universities, and which can therefore be translated into financial capital, for instance through employment. The way accents are perceived by *standard* language users can in turn mean positioning and 'othering' by race, socio-economic status, gender and geographic origin (Bourdieu & Thompson, 1991; Trudgill, 1974). This can result in typecasting and discrimination, especially notice-able in education (Donnelly, Baratta & Gamsu, 2019). This resonates with Chen (1997), who summarises the field of sociology of language as starting from the perspective that language has value in and between social groups. Expanding on this, Gerhards (2014) shows that languages are evaluated differently in terms of their desirability. As an example, he describes English as prestigious *transnational* linguistic capital, or as a resource to participate in the globalisation process, whereas other languages and language varieties are evaluated as less valuable. Angermuller and Glady sum up perspectives on language, formulated in the field of sociology of language, by arguing that "the social is realised in large parts through linguistic practices, and that linguistic practices are social practices" (2017, pp. 174–175, our translation). Sociological studies of language are therefore about situations where diverse languages come into contact with one another, and about the relation-ship between the larger social and political contexts where such language contacts occur (Chen, 1997). Consequently, Angmueller & Glady (2017) conceive languages as "a human activity that forms part of a fund of linguistic resources that can be used to realise social practices", a position also adopted by educationalists and policy makers (e.g. Busch, 2012; Council of Europe, 2001; 2018). This understanding of language as a social value that can be enacted and used in social situ-ations also informs broader concepts in the field of applied linguistics. The term *plurilingualism*, for example, describes how a linguistic reper-toire is "constructed as individuals pursue their lives, it is a reflection of their social paths" (Coste et al., 2009, p. 17) and is understood to be related to group affiliations and identity.

Language linked to identity and language groups

While plurilingualism, as a term, denotes the uses of different languages and language varieties in society, research studies in applied linguistics and social psychology have framed languages, and the way they are used, as an important source of identification and belonging (for much-cited examples, see Norton, 2014; Dörnyei & Ushioda, 2009; Cummins et al., 2006; Blackledge, 2004;). Norton and McKinney, for example, propose language as a tool through which "relationships and identities are defined, negotiated, and resisted" (2011, p. 77). Thus, relationships and identities are shaped through contacts between speakers and groups of speakers of different languages and language varieties (Vetter, 2015, p. 107). Such language groups have been described as 'layered' (Blommaert, 2006), as they are neither static, fixed nor bounded, but dynamic, in flux and overlapping with others group allegiances (Meier, 2017; Darquennes, 2015; Vetter, 2015; Cruickshank, 2014; May, 2014; Blommaert, 2006). Identities are contested or resisted, or conflict can occur, when groups who use two languages or language varieties come into contact in "settings whose conditions are controversially evaluated by people who are involved" (Haarmann, 1990, p. 2–3). Language in contested settings and conditions can therefore become a deeply political element in the struggle for identity, belonging and social cohesion. Language identities can be contested, for instance in colonial settings (e.g. Atindogbé & Ebongue, 2019; Sengupta, 2018), in settings of urban multilingualism (e.g. Blackledge, 2004; Blommaert, 2006), and in education (e.g. Cummins et al., 2006); often these contexts intersect and overlap. The way languages and identities are evaluated depends to a large extent on language norms, or what is deemed normal language use and behaviour in a given society, as described next.

Language norms

Speech communities share not only a language but also social and evaluative language norms, according to pioneering work by sociolinguist William Labov (1972). The way language norms shape our values, attitudes and social lives is also studied with the help of language socialisation theories that build on the premise that "language is the central dimension of socialisation" (Ganek et al., 2019, p. 140), and as part of this socialisation, young people learn which languages, language varieties and styles play what role in which social situations. Language socialisation has, therefore, been defined as a "meaningful action that occurs routinely in everyday life, is widely shared by members of the group, has developed over time, and carries normative expectations about how it should be done" (Moore, 2005, p. 72). Language norms are a reflection of prevailing ideologies that inform societal expectations related to languages (Duff & Talmy, 2011). Blommaert (2006) described language and *linguistic cultures*, which are enacted during such actions, as referred to above, as shaping societal norms. In many parts of the world, language norms are also influenced by the one nation-one language doctrine associated with the nation building projects of the late 19th and early 20th centuries (Wright, 2004). Theoretical and policy conceptualisations have not been immune to this, and their treatment of language has been critiqued as instrumentalist (Riera-Gil, 2019; Pennycook, 2001; Tollefson, 1991), insofar as the majority, or more powerful, language is typically associated with successful participation, opportunities and social justice (Riera-Gil, 2019), without taking social hierarchy, power structures and social justice (e.g. Pennycook, 2001; Tollefson, 1991) – or other languages (Cummins, 2019; Ortega, 2014; Gogolin, 1994) – into consideration. It is often argued that such unquestioned language norms, and simplistic understandings of language in society, policy and education (Riera-Gil, 2019; Gajo, 2014; Ricento, 2014; Blommaert, 2006), contrast sharply with the de facto multilingualism that is found in societies and institutions, as well as in individuals (Lengyel, 2017). This strand of literature shows that norms, values and attitudes are subjective, often based on popular assumptions that are taken for granted. In addition, it suggests that such norms inform perceptions of social status, legitimacy and inclusion. The concept of "a language" may therefore seem "banally obvious" at first sight, but it is an "invented construct" (NicCraith, 2000, p. 402) that is political in nature.

Languages as political and contested

NicCraith (2000, pp. 402–403) emphasises that "the status of a language or dialect is dependent on the political status of its speakers", pointing to the hierarchical nature of language negotiations in language contact and language conflict situations. Blommaert (2006, p. 511) points out that linguistic ethnographers concur that "human communication through language displays meaningful metalevel inscriptions, adding a layer of sociopolitical, ideological meaning to the event". Ideology is defined as "the cultural system of ideas about social and linguistic relationships, together with their loading of moral and political interests" (Irvine, 1989, p. 255). In other words, language in its spoken or written form is not a neutral element in communication but instead indexes multiple belongings, such as generation, educational background, social class, ethnicity, and geographic affiliation, and is therefore "evaluative, relational, socially positioned, invested with interests, and subject to contestation and dominance" (p. 511). As such, languages are inherently political and a site of struggle (Sarroub & Quadros, 2014), interlinked with sociopolitical and historical factors (Kumaravadivelu, 2005, p. 72).

Researchers from various fields, therefore, emphasise the ideological dimension of languages. Such ideologies underpin norms and behaviour with respect to which languages and language groups are privileged over others (see languages and social hierarchies: May, 2014; Ortega, 2014; Blommaert, 2006), whether languages are linked to territory or to people who use them (see language essentialism: McIntosh, 2005), ways in which different groups in a society respond to multilingualism (see power struggles connected to language pluralities: Gagnon, 2006) and the many sites in which language is central to social justice issues based on the above (see, for example, Avineri, Graham, Johnson, Riner & Rosa, 2019; Sengupta, 2018). Ideologically informed debates about how languages ought to be used therefore overlap with debates about access to education and health provision, as well as in relation to social activism, race discourses and language policies. In terms of relevance to social cohesion, such links to ideologically driven perceptions of languages mean that "language often develops into a significant symbol of social conflict, even if it is not the direct cause of the conflict" (Darquennes, 2015, p. 12). Language conflict, according to Darquennes, can have a surface and a deep structure. Thus, debates in situations of conflict might focus on languages and language use (surface), when the actual issue is about political, historical or ideological struggles (deep structure). The focus on language might, therefore, distract the attention from the other sociopolitical motivations behind an assumed language conflict.

In his significant article, Darquennes (2015) suggests that the concept of language conflict consists of different dimensions, namely linguistic strife, conflicting language ideologies and contested language varieties. Language conflict might occur where language varieties pertaining notionally to the same language (e.g. standard language, dialects and accents), different regional languages (e.g. French and English in Canada, French, German, Italian and Romansh in Switzerland) and dominant and minority languages (e.g. official and indigenous or migrant languages) come into contact. Social tensions may be associated with language conflict caused by conflicting language ideologies, power aspirations and sometimes long-held grievances or historic antipathies. In such language contact situations, "language conflict is pre-programmed, yet might not always be visible", Darquennes (2015, p. 13) argues. Of particular relevance for our project is his recommendation to explore the mutual influences between personal language choices and ideologies, and societal conflict:

> Combined research on interpersonal and societal language conflict would be an interesting exercise in merging the different

views on "language" and "society" that – since the early days of sociolinguistics and the sociology of language – mark the usually more macro-oriented approaches to societal and the more micro-oriented approaches to interpersonal language questions (including questions related to language conflict).

(Darquennes, 2015, p. 23)

In this book, we respond to Darquennes' suggestion, as our project was designed to bridge between micro (intergroup) and macro (socio-political) orientations. We would like to stress, however, that our starting point is not language conflict (for that, see, for example, Darquennes, 2015; Vetter, 2015), but the assumption that language contact and language competences are intertwined with people's experiences of social cohesion, of belonging, of being, in societies with complex push–pull factors in their allegiances. Languages are not only a concern for people who use and negotiate them in their daily lives, in a kind of bottom-up fashion, language use, language norms and allegiances are also influenced by decision makers through language policies or language management in varied ways.

Language management in society

Various disciplines have an interest in how languages are managed in society, as they focus on issues of language policy and planning. From a sociolinguistic position (e.g. Goundar, 2017) language policy and planning is "concerned with the creation, interpretation and appropriation of policy on language status, corpus or acquisition in particular contexts" (p. 86). From a sociology of language perspective, language policy and planning issues arise, or might arise, through language contact and possible ensuing conflict emerging through contextual and ideological factors. Darquennes summarises that "to correct, neutralize, or de-emotionalize a situation of language conflict, language policy and planning come into play" (2015, p. 17). Language policy and planning is therefore one of the core aspects in any consideration of languages and the establishment or maintenance of social cohesion in or between different language groups. However, whether or not particularly top-level language management initiatives (e.g. official policies) are successful "depends on the willingness of the population to accept the measures in different domains of society as they are implemented from above, and to complement them with grassroots initiatives 'from below'" (Darquennes, 2015, p. 20). Sociologists of language thus view language management as an interplay between "top-down" decision making by institutions or authorities (macro), and the every-day language use of individuals and groups (micro) (Nekvapil & Sherman, 2015, p. 2). This is important here, as top-down language planning needs to take into consideration societal sensitivities, practices and norms. Darquennes warns that a careful analysis of the language conflict situation, including underlying inequalities and social tensions, is required to move forward towards social cohesion through language policy and planning.

In contexts of immigration and globalisation, various political ideologies are invoked in the name of social integration and how languages should be managed. Central to this stance is "linguistic nationalism" which equates competence in the majority language with "allegiance towards the new society and acceptance of the nation's core values" (Kalocsányiová, 2018, p. 2). Language policies and planning based on such concepts can conjure up group togetherness and discursive symbolism based on one particular language, and 'othering' of those who are not seen to belong, and who are assumed to share different values and norms (Kalocsányiová, 2018). Along these lines, Wodak found that increasingly, "language competence [in the official dominant language] has acquired the status of a key gatekeeper – providing access for some and rejecting it for others" (2012, p. 230). Some may see this as a natural requirement for social integration (a term to which we will return later), while others may question such exclusive practices based on unequal power relations between those who are able to meet the language requirements and others who struggle to do this.

This is related to a major issue that surfaces in the literature about language policy and planning, namely the tension between nationalist and pluralist views, and who is seen as legitimate in a given society and who is not. Jenson (2019, p. 3), who understands pluralism and social cohesion as positively correlated, presents pluralism as a particular *shared value* held by a proportion of a given population as an expression of a shared respect for human diversity, which in turn is formed in a particular context. Schiffman (1996, p. 5) described shared values as related to linguistic culture (see also Blommaert, 2006), which can be expressed by "a set of behaviors, assumptions, cultural forms, prejudices, folk belief systems, attitudes, stereotypes, ways of thinking about language, and religio-historical circumstances associated with a particular language". Jenson argues that policy makers, through institutions, legislatures, courts, schools and the media, as well as societies, through cultural habits and norms, can both be instrumental in steering shared values. There is some consensus in sociology of language that language status and shared values are influenced through this interplay between top-down (institutional/macro) and bottom-up (societal/micro) forces (Jenson, 2019; Nekvapil & Sherman, 2015; Schiffman, 1996).

When several languages are present in a social context, language policy and social integration debates are generally characterised by divergent norms and beliefs about how languages should be organised in a society. Stolle (2013) offers an overview of possible language policy dispositions in multilingual societies: (1) a monolingual, homogeneous society is conducive to social cohesion (enabling participation through linguistic assimilation); (2) linguistic communities can successfully coexist side by side (enabling groups to maintain their cultures through multiculturalism and tolerance towards multilingualism); and (3) socially cohesive societies require meaningful contact between different linguistic groups (enabling inter-group contact through inter-, transculturalism associated with societal integration of languages). Researchers associated with interethnic contact theory (see, for example, Amin, 2002; Allport, 1954) and social cohesion in ethnically diverse societies (see, for example, Cantle 2012) generally support the view that Stolle's third policy disposition is conducive to social cohesion, enabled by meaningful interaction, transcultural contacts, by breaking down segregation and advancing integration, "without threatening existing conceptions of ourselves" (Cantle, 2012, p. 206). However, expectations of how society should be organised can vary within communities, but also across countries and cultures. For instance, Chan et al. (2006, 293) highlight that successful social cohesion measures are context sensitive, insofar as what may promote social cohesion in a modern capitalist society, may be of less relevance in another type of society that might value other forms of social organisation. Amin's work also relates to Stolle's (2013) third point, as he postulates that policy in contested or ethnically diverse territories needs to enable conditions "where engagement with strangers in common activity disrupts easy labelling of the stranger as enemy and initiates new attachments" (Amin, 2002, p. 970). From a governance perspective, Kearns and Forrest add that "the city of diversity and difference is also the city of division and fragmentation" and that "the achievement of greater social cohesion requires an awareness of these differences and of the tensions between them" (2000, pp. 1013–1014). The management of such conditions, partly through language policy and planning, must be acknowledged as hugely complex and deeply embedded in diverse contexts and cultures. Our book, thus, aims to reveal insights into the languages component that may be of use for policy makers entrusted with managing diversity and difference.

One important tool to manage languages in society is language education. Education as a site for language management is investigated by applied linguistics (e.g. through studies in language learning), sociolinguistics (e.g. looking into different uses of languages in education), sociology of language (e.g. by focusing on language contact and conflict), language socialisation (e.g. by identifying schools as generating norms through language use), and by language policy and planning (investigating the policy decisions about languages being used, taught and studied in education). It is recognised that language acquisition and language status planning (Wright, 2004; Ricento, 2014) can be implemented through language curricula (Reich & Krumm, 2013; Coyle, Holmes & King, 2009) for instance. Language hierarchies and norms are influenced through languages that are prioritised (or restricted) as languages of teaching and learning, or included (or excluded) as foreign and additional languages within the curriculum (Wright, 2004). Specifically, language acquisition planning is about managing linguistic resources and how they are distributed in a society, while language status planning is about influencing the perceived importance of relevant languages. Language management in schools is therefore a principal concern for any investigation of access to resources, and shared (or diverging) norms and values – these are both central tenets of social cohesion as we will explore later. In multilingual settings, political and educational debates often centre around curricular languages that are imposed top-down (typically official languages of teaching and learning, as well as foreign and classical languages), and any other languages that learners bring to and use in their education (bottom-up).

Thus, the educational system can influence linguistic norms and status, by offering prestige languages (Smala, Bergas Paz & Lingard, 2013; Hu, 2008) sought after as positioning capital, for instance by educated cosmopolitan classes, or by suppressing first languages other than the main language of teaching and learning, on the assumption that this creates equal access and unity (Cummins, 2019; Fouka, 2016; Kioko, Ndung'u, Njoroge & Mutiga, 2014). Policies of first-language suppression are often based on the premise that language heterogeneity necessarily leads to conflict (see, for example, Nelde, 1997). Kioko et al. (2014, p. 4) locate the problem not in the existence of many languages, in a school in their case, but in the fact that "the many languages simply communicate animosities that stem from social, political and economic issues in the nation". Educational settings, therefore, might also have a surface engagement with languages that hides deeper political and ideological issues.

From this strand of literature we can learn that, through the interplay of top-down and bottom-up language policy and planning, social cohesion can be influenced, by steering language norms and status. However, what type of language policies may be more conducive to social integration and social cohesion remains a contested debate. We now turn to the concepts and theories discussed in social cohesion literature.

Conceptualisation of social cohesion and links to languages

S*ocial cohesion* is a concept that has been studied in different disciplinary perspectives within social sciences, above all in the fields of sociology, political science, psychology and social psychology (Schiefer & van der Noll, 2017; Chan et al., 2006). An exploration of what social cohesion might constitute often focuses on the relationship between society and its members, as well as general patterns of behaviour. Green et al. (2006) remind us that social cohesion cannot be understood in a void, as the dynamics are highly contextualised. Social psychologists seek to understand factors that influence social behaviour by focusing on interpersonal relationships situated in social contexts, while sociologists seek to understand process and systems related to social stability and division (Branscombe & Baron, 2017; Allport, 1954). Green et al. (2006) succinctly sum up the problematic nature of social cohesion:

> For most people, in most societies, social cohesion is probably a desirable state, so long as it is based on equality, or at least relative equality, of access to goods, opportunities and power. But such situations have rarely been achieved, historically, without social conflicts and struggle. Such is the paradox of social cohesion.
>
> (Green et al., 2006, p. 10)

This paradox may be the reason why the construct of social cohesion is widely described as ambiguous, complex, multidimensional and difficult to define (see, for example, Kearns & Forrest, 2000; Schiefer & van der Noll, 2017, p. 579). To start with, the terms *social cohesion* and *social integration* are not clearly delineated. In some of the literature *social integration* is used in contexts of immigration, denoting the respective social and system (civic) integration that enable immigrants or newcomers to participate in what is often referred to as a 'host' society (Cheong, Edwards, Goulbourne & Solomos, 2007). Some authors (Giardello, 2014; Chan et al., 2006; Lockwood, 1999) found that social cohesion is sometimes treated as part of social integration, suggesting that social integration comprises both social integration or cohesion (micro) and civic or system integration (macro). Furthermore, social cohesion and social capital are also used synonymously on occasion (see for example Crowley & Hickman, 2008), as respective explanations of those terms overlap. In policy discourses the term *community cohesion* is often used (Worley, 2005), while in academic circles *social cohesion* is used to denote a similar concept to community cohesion (a point made by Green, Preston & Janmaat, 2006).

Our work was guided by a couple of recent and very helpful sociological reviews on the topic of social cohesion (Schiefer & van der Noll, 2017; Chan et al., 2006). In addition, we also draw on social capital approaches developed by leading sociologists (Cantle, 2006; Paxton, 2002; Lin, 2001; Putnam, 2000; Coleman, 1988; Bourdieu, 1986; Granovetter, 1983, 1973) and key concepts such as imagined communities (Anderson, 1983). On the basis of this and related literature, we developed a working definition for the purpose of our project as follows.

Defining social cohesion

According to Cheong et al. (2007, p. 29), "social cohesion is used generally to refer to common values and purpose in a society, including a sense of belonging and solidarity for people from diverse backgrounds". In turn, social capital is described as "traits of individual trust, tolerance, and civic participation which are said to underpin the relations of reciprocity in well-functioning participative communities" (Green et al., 2006, p. 3). Holland (2009, p. 340) defines social capital as "the values people hold and the resources that they can access, which both result in and are the result of collective and socially negotiated ties and relationships". Whereas Putnam defines social capital as the "features of social life – networks, norms and trust – that enable participants to act together more effectively to pursue shared objectives" (Putnam, 1996, p. 1). Such a conceptualisation seems to suggest that social capital is a 'cure' for lack of social cohesion. There is a consensus, according to Chan et al. (2006), that dimensions of social capital, namely social networks, resources, trust, and norms and values, are also dimensions of social cohesion (Chan et al., 2006, p. 292). Some of these concepts are shared with social psychologists (Chan et al., 2006), specifically, the interest "in ways in which our thoughts, feelings, and actions are *influenced* by the social environments in which we find ourselves – by other people or our thoughts about them" (Branscombe & Baron, 2017, p. 20, original emphasis). In addition to concepts such as social norms, belonging, trust and behaviour as key dimensions of social cohesion, in our book we are also concerned with structure or systemic questions of social organisation and stability, which sociologists have also explored with regard to social cohesion (Chan et al. (2006).

There is a long tradition of scholars interested in the role of language(s) in social cohesion. While sociologist Pierre Bourdieu (1986) considered language, especially in social elites, as a means to develop social networks and gain economic and social advantages, other theorists in this field are also concerned with language, but tend to view it in rather simplistic terms, as shown by Schiefer & van der Noll (2017). They found that the social cohesion literature they reviewed tends to associate a common language (alongside culture and traditions) with bonding and identification in a nation, while those with other languages, cultures, or religions struggle to participate in a given society. While we acknowledge such views of the role of language(s) at a national or nation-building level (Schiefer & van der Noll, 2017), or related to socio-economic advantages (Bourdieu, 1986), we also embrace Chan et al.'s (2006, p. 291) dimensions of social cohesion as containing *objective* and *subjective* components. Objective dimensions refer to actual social networks, participation and behaviour, whereas subjective dimensions denote norms, feelings and attitudes. As established in the previous section, languages are not neutral, and they are subjectively evaluated. This suggests that a purely objective and instrumental view of how language enables social participation may be limited. In the following, we will unpack each of these dimensions and relate them to languages where appropriate.

Social networks and behaviour

In Schiefer & van der Noll's (2017, p. 584) broad analysis, social networks are found to be about "the functionality and problem solving capacity of societies", comprising connections among individuals (see also Putnam, 2000). Social networks are described as behaviour manifestations (Chan et al., 2006; Friedkin, 2004) and as manifestation of relationships (Schiefer & van der Noll, 2017). In sociological research, such observable and measurable social connections and relationships that are manifest and observable at group level are important indicators of social cohesion. For Chan et al. (2006, p. 290) this means observable "acts of belonging, trust, cooperation and help".

Social network research distinguishes between the quality (weak and strong) and the direction (horizontal and vertical) of networks. 'Horizontal' focuses on the interactions among individuals and groups in society who establish links within and between social groups, whereas 'vertical' refers to the relationship between the state and society at large (Chan et al. 2006). Vertical ties are therefore associated with ties across levels of institutional power as well as social hierarchies.

In horizontal terms, people can build bonds or strong ties (Cheong et al., 2007; Lin, 2001) to people to whom they feel emotionally close, as well as wider networks of acquaintances (often called weak or bridging ties) to reach beyond people's close-knit groups (Granovetter, 1983, 1973). These weak ties are conducive to establishing bridges between diverse groups, as weak ties can "bring together people from different social and cultural backgrounds" (Field, 2003, p. 66). Weak ties can therefore also act as bridges between otherwise separate strong-tie networks or groups and are often deemed crucial for social cohesion in societies (see, for example, Lin, 2001; Granovetter, 1983, 1973). Strong-tie networks are characterised by "intensity, intimacy, frequency of contacts, acknowledged obligations, and provision of reciprocal services" (Lin 2001, p. 67), from which individuals can benefit importantly in practical and emotional terms. Typically, family ties are considered strong ties (Lin, 2001), and Coleman (1988, p. 113) stresses the importance of the ties between children and parents (horizontal), as well as people's relations with the "institutions of the community", such as schools (vertical). It is important to note that strong-tie networks can not only manifest themselves as close-knit groups of family and friends or support groups, but they can also take on exclusive, separatist or nationalist characteristics, including gang culture or criminal behaviour (Field, 2003), and can be detrimental to social cohesion by undermining stability, solidarity and security. Such aspects of social cohesion describe systemic and structural dimensions, and are particularly important when investigating contexts where diversity and difference are present (Chan et al., 2006). Chan et al. warn that the presence of large weak networks, as well as strong social networks, alone need not imply a high level of social cohesion, since in a highly ethnically segregated society individuals may maintain large social networks with members of the same ethnic group with no inter-ethnic social ties at all (2006, p. 292). Of interest for this book are the ways linguistic resources, as discussed in the first part of this chapter, are used – or not used – to build different types of social networks in settings that are linguistically diverse.

Linguistic and other resources

In many sociological texts, a socially cohesive society might be described as one that, among other aspects, is "bound together by the same language, culture and traditions" (Schiefer & van der Noll, 2017, p. 584). Thus, a shared language could be viewed as a resource that enables interaction and participation within and across linguistic groups. Our focus here is to unpack this rather broad statement with the help of applied linguistic research. Both Blommaert (2006) and Ricento (2014) referred to languages as a resource itself that is distributed unevenly in society, with some languages and language varieties enabling access to some resources but not others. Riera-Gil (2019) found that in policy texts, similar to the statement above, majority languages are often constructed as a necessary shared resource that is required to access practical and material networks associated with social mobility within a society, whereas minority languages are constructed as a means to express identity and culture, without having explicit value as a resource for social mobility. As social networks are built – presumably through the use of one or more languages – other material and immaterial resources become potentially available, horizontally from individual networks (Putnam, 2000; Coleman, 1988; Bourdieu, 1986), and vertically between individuals and institutions (Cantle, 2006; Chan et al., 2006). Schiefer & van der Noll (2017) refer to the distributive dimension of resources as a dimension of social cohesion, which encompasses "the (un)equal distribution of physical, economic, social, and cultural resources" (p. 585). Unequal distribution of resources, both at societal level and in individual networks, in turn, can lead to "isolation of individuals or groups from the social and cultural life" (p. 591). Following this argument, in a socially cohesive society members would have relatively equal access to resources. The authors describe the type of resources that may be gained through networks, as material or immaterial, including "for example, employment, income, education, health care, social welfare, and legal means" (p. 591). An aspect that will play an important role in this book is the role of language as tool – and a resource in itself – that enables social relationships and access to further resources, an aspect that has not been fully explored in social cohesion literature. While social networks and (linguistic) resources can be described as objective or observable dimensions, we now turn to invisible or subjective dimensions of social cohesion.

Norms and values

Similar to definitions offered in the language socialisation literature (see, for example, Ganek et al., 2019), the social cohesion literature often describes social norms as based on subjective values and understandings, as well as on beliefs of how things should be done. Thus, norms are related to a set of ideas or a world view, which Schiefer & van der Noll (2017, p. 585) refer to as an "ideational dimension [that] comprises cognitive and affective facets such as norms, values, and identification". In Bicchieri's (2005) words, norms include "the language a society speaks, the embodiment of its values and collective desires, the secure guide in the uncertain lands we all traverse, the common practices that hold human groups together" (p. ix). Shared norms are based on shared collective values, beliefs, traditions, culture and lifestyles (Schiefer & van der Noll, 2017), from which social obligations are derived (Kearns & Forrest, 2000). Value consensus and common goals, according to Schiefer & van der Noll (2017), are often assumed to smooth social interactions based on mutually accepted norms. Chan et al. (2006, p. 292) make the important point that social cohesion does not require any particular type of values, as long as they are shared in a society. Shared values could be based on a preference for "hierarchically structured power relations and deference to authorities" (Schiefer & van der Noll, 2017, p. 597), or on pluralism and liberal values (Jenson, 2019). Both could be viewed as facilitators of social networks.

Trust and common goals are also considered part of the subjective side of social cohesion referred to by Chan et al. (2006). Specifically, trust in people, groups and institutions (Putnam, 2000; Paxton, 2002), as well as common goals (Schiefer & van der Noll, 2017), is seen as part of shared values and acceptance of social norms. This leads Schiefer and van der Noll to conclude that instead of a value consensus, a society that aims to be socially cohesive "should promote (and value) the constructive coexistence of individuals who differ in their values" (2017, p. 590). Attitudes also form part of this subjective value system as they steer, for instance, the willingness to help or participate in society (Chan et al., 2006), which is the precondition for observable social behaviour. Social behaviour conducive to social cohesion is therefore not necessarily only about smooth and harmonious relationships, but also about "open-ended engagement, vibrant opposition and negotiation", as outlined by Cheong et al. (2007, p. 40). Furthermore, subjective value systems that underlie and inform social action and engagement are not understood as fixed, but as dynamic. For instance social psychologists argue that meaningful cooperation across language boundaries can result in more positive attitudes towards the group one engages with (e.g. Branscombe & Baron, 2017; Taylor, Peplau & Sears, 2006), which indicates that attitudes can change due to experiences.

For the purposes of this book, we therefore embrace the notion that the ideational and subjective dimensions which are conducive to social cohesion comprise shared norms (a set of ideas), based on values (including trust, beliefs and common goals), that underlie attitudes to acting in society. In addition, we acknowledge that the subjective component of social cohesion might also consist of feelings, particularly a feeling or sense of belonging or affiliation, as described next.

Sense of belonging to a group

One key concept in the theoretical construct of social cohesion is a 'sense of belonging'. A sense of belonging describes "the feeling [of being] attached to or identify with the social entity (a group, region, country, or a transnational entity such as the European Union) for social cohesion" (Schiefer & van der Noll, 2017, p. 588). Sense of belonging can therefore have horizontal and vertical directionality, as people can feel they belong to small local groups, as well as to larger, more abstract or imagined social entities, such as institutions and states, with whom they feel they share values and norms. Kearns & Forrest (2000) understand such attachment and belonging in terms of concrete emotional, spatial, civic and practical belonging. Importantly, they view belonging as evident at local ("Neighbourhood/Interurban"), regional ("City/City-region") and national ("National/Interurban") levels. The sense of territorial belonging is often nuanced and multi-layered, as "a city can consist of socially cohesive but increasingly divided neighbourhoods" (Kearns & Forrest, 2000, p. 2013), echoing Chan et al.'s (2006) concerns of ethnic segregation despite the presence of extensive social networks. In his key work *Imagined Communities – Reflections on the Origins and Spread of Nationalism*, political scientist and historian Benedict Anderson describes sense of imaginary belonging to a national group as a potentially deep, horizontal comradeship, emphasising perceived equality (Anderson, 1983, p. 14). Imaginary belonging is also a concern of social psychologists (e.g. Branscombe & Baron, 2017; Taylor, Peplau & Sears, 2006). They argue that affiliation with certain groups, including national and linguistic groups, is important for identification, even if we do not personally know many of the co-members of this group. Language, according to Anderson (1983), constitutes a central means to feel solidarity and belonging with a group of people, who are sometimes unknown to the person who feels affiliated with that imagined larger language group or nation. This means that belonging can be concrete or imagined, which resonates closely with Pavlenko & Norton's view of the role of imagined communities in language learning:

> we humans are capable, through our imagination, of perceiving a connection with people beyond our immediate social networks. Our orientation toward such imagined communities might have just as much impact on our current identities and learning as direct involvement in communities of our everyday life.
>
> (2007, p. 670)

In the reviews on social cohesion we consulted (particularly Chan et al., 2006; Schiefer & van der Noll, 2017), majority languages are also associated with a more symbolic sense of belonging. Schiefer and van der Noll (2017) mention the majority language as a basis for linguistic nationalism and national pride, based on the assumption that acquiring and using the language would indicate shared values. A lack of the majority language in this scenario is associated with exclusion, as those not proficient in the majority language would be perceived as not belonging to "us" (Schiefer & van der Noll, 2017).

In more recent years, we have come to understand that the sense of belonging to a group might be disconnected from territories, as globalisation has brought "new forms of social cleavages" (Chan et al., 2006, p. 279) through international economic activity, the Internet, and voluntary or forced migration and geographic mobility. We suspect that social cohesion, understood as a societal attribute (cohesiveness of a specific society as a whole, as described by Chan et al. 2006), and a sense of belonging as an individual experience, might sometimes be at odds through these new cleavages. In Schiefer & van der Noll's words, it is possible that "citizens turn to smaller identity-establishing social units such as ethnicity or religion which subsequently further fragments a society's unity" (2017, p. 589), or to transnational and diasporic groups, enabled through the digital revolution, with diverse affiliations potentially in conflict with one another (Kearns & Forrest, 2000).

A sense of belonging, therefore, was traditionally connected to geographical and local ties, but is increasingly divorced from such space restrictions. This has implications for language as the site of belonging. Language socialisation, traditionally part of the geographical and local emerging sense of belonging, can now happen independent of physical spaces, due to the before-mentioned globalisation flows. This means that ideology, social representations, shared norms, practices and identities are also a concern of language socialisation perspectives (Schieffelin & Ochs, 1986), as diverse language (and ideology) socialisation might occur in the same geographical space. Authors working under the banner of language socialisation tend to agree that language socialisation is about production and reproduction of an (imagined) language community, as well as about the dynamic changes and transformations of social reality that re-define belonging and cohesion (Friedman, 2010; Watson-Gegeo, 2004; Garret & Baquedano-López, 2002). Having established the dimensions of social cohesion that are of relevance for our project, we round off this chapter with a summary that leads us to the next chapter.

Towards a transdisciplinary framework

In this chapter, we reviewed literature from the broad field of applied linguistics, social psychology and sociology, as well as from related fields, with a special focus on where they overlap in a transdisciplinary way. This literature helped us define and operationalise the concepts of language and social cohesion, and initial interlinkages between them, for the purpose of our study.

Through the literature, we have established that languages can be defined as layered, based potentially on several standard languages and language varieties. The functions of languages have been described as instrumental, affective or symbolic, insofar as languages can be used to participate in society and gain benefits. Languages also allow affective identification with linguistic groups, and they have symbolic power and status, which positions a person in a social hierarchy or societal power structure, alongside other characteristics. Language groups have also been defined as layered or overlapping, dynamic and changing, depending on context and over the course of a life time. Languages have also been shown to have a political and ideological dimension, associated with language norms, indicating that that there is a shared or diverging language behaviour that is expected or deemed normal in a given society. Deviations from this, which are inevitable, since languages and language groups are evaluated differently by different groups, can lead to social tensions and divisions. Attitudes, and resulting behaviour, towards a language group can be positively affected by concrete meaningful contact with members of other language groups, or by more symbolic meaning that is associated with a language, as suggested by social psychologists. According to the scoping literature reviewed in this chapter, language norms and attitudes can be influenced through formal language policy, issued by institutions and authorities, as well as by grassroots language practices in society. Tensions can occur when formal policies and grassroots expectations and practices do not match. Moreover, we established that languages, as defined earlier, are complex phenomena interacting with a variety of social cohesion aspects.

In the literature on social cohesion we reviewed in this chapter, languages feature primarily as a requirement for the population to develop a competence in the majority language, without which groups tend to be excluded from the majority society. While literature based on applied linguistics questions this simple, but arguably common sense, correlation, the literature on social cohesion offers extremely useful concepts that formed a basis for our project. A key concept associated with social cohesion is social networks, which can be weak or strong. According to this theory, social networks to one group alone do not indicate social cohesion, but it is the existence of simultaneous weak and strong networks that is an indicator of social cohesion in a given context. Languages are described as social resources by applied linguists; therefore, we expect languages, in the form of language repertoires, to act as instruments that facilitate such (multiple) networks within and across language groups. Social networks, and resources that can be accessed, are considered objective – or observable – features of social cohesion. The literature also stresses the importance of underlying subjective – or invisible – features of social cohesion. These are norms and values, as well as sense of belonging. These two dimensions, which are considered aspects of social cohesion by social psychologists and sociologists, are also commonly used in applied linguistics. In the latter field, the concepts of language norms and language identification are typically examined by sociolinguistics and language education researchers respectively. Even though we treated the concepts rather separately in this chapter, the overlaps that became visible at this stage (see Table 2.1) encouraged us to identify wider literature to explore these linkages between the concepts and their dimensions in greater detail.

Table 2.1 Transdisciplinary framework based on scoping literature

Level of analysis	Theme	Sub-themes
Contexts where languages and social cohesion interact	Language use in society	Languages and language varieties used to communicate and form identities
	Language education	Languages included in curricula; type of language education; language practices
	Language policy and planning	Language regulations that encourage linguistic diversity or monolingualism; language as a proxy for other problems
Objective dimensions of interaction between language and social cohesion	Language as a resource	As a tool for social participation; as distributed in society; as a source of status
	Languages used to develop social networks	Weak, strong, horizontal, vertical, multiple ties
	Languages in social cohesion breakdown	Lack of access to networks; resources; belonging
Subjective dimensions of the role languages play in social cohesion	Language group affiliations	Languages as markers of identity; languages used to generate dominant language and imagined affiliations
	Language norms and attitudes	Languages perceived as a problem; local vs global orientations

The overarching dimensions (and sub-themes) we established in this chapter are summarised in Table 2.1, and served as a theory-informed (deductive) framework for our thematic analysis.

These aspects of languages and social cohesion form our framework for the thematic analysis that guided our systematic literature review, as well as provided search words, as described in Chapter 3. The 285 articles included in our systematic review, and presented in Chapter 4, allowed us not only to confirm aspects already discussed in this chapter, but also to expand and further develop this framework to include aspects and components based on evidence identified in the wider literature. In addition, this analytical work contributes, in conjunction with the systematic literature review presented in Chapters 3 and 4, to an expanded transdisciplinary understanding of the possible linkages between languages and social cohesion (see Figure 5.1). As will be seen in Chapter 5, based on the analysis and interpretation of this combined body of literature, we have developed questions that help explore these linkages in particular contexts (see Table 5.1). These questions are the first step towards a potential practical impact of our insights in contexts where languages and social cohesion are interrogated.

3 Studies linking languages and social cohesion

Developing a body of research

In order to answer the research question, which was about ways in which languages are associated with social cohesion in academic articles, we needed to develop a research design that would help us first identify and then analyse relevant articles. Following on from Chapter 2, where we established key concepts and how they are understood from different disciplinary perspectives, in this chapter we introduce the transdisciplinary approach that guided our systematic literature review and analysis. Furthermore, we describe how we identified 285 articles that evidence links between languages and social cohesion. The literature search followed Moher et al.'s (2009) PRIMSA protocol which allows for a transparent recount of steps. A quantitative description of the body of relevant articles we identified as relevant is given in the following, including the journals in which they were published, research contexts, and type of articles.

Importantly, a comprehensive and complete list of references for the 285 articles we included in our final corpus are available in an EndNote Library external to this book. This is freely available to access (Meier, Smala & Lawson, 2021, https://data.mendeley.com/datasets/ydtms99mjm/3). Following on from the quantitative description of the body of literature, we outline the thematic approach we used to develop the deeper insights into this data set, whose results we present in Chapter 4.

Transdisciplinary approach

Transdisciplinary approaches can be understood as researchers immersing themselves in an "ecology of ideas" (Montuori, 2013, p. 46). Montuori's (2013) definition of transdisciplinarity served as a useful guide for our study.

DOI: 10.4324/9781003120384-3

A transdisciplinary view, informed by systems and complex thought, addresses the larger whole, the context, the relationships and interactions, and the many dimensions or system levels that emerge in the process – whether the brain, individual person, group, community, nation, and the global context. The task – and art – of transdisciplinary research, is to assess to what extent these different system levels are sources of pertinent information.

(p. 48)

This approach aspires to grasp the complexity of societally relevant problems (Hirsch Hadorn et al., 2008), "by creating new conceptual, theoretical, and methodological approaches that move beyond discipline–specific perspectives" (Bibri, 2021, p. 3). Our transdisciplinary review, thus, aimed to present a detailed analysis, synthesis and reconstruction of ideas, as well as a critical evaluation and discussion of the identifiable research, comprising a range of research designs that address the topic under scrutiny.

Transdisciplinarity is understood, on the one hand, as working in the space between disciplines where they overlap, as described in Chapter 2. On the other hand, transdisciplinarity can be a collaboration between academics and interest groups, based in industry, politics or education, working together to explore and develop understandings of real-world phenomena (Hirsch Hadorn et al., 2008). In this book, and for our data collection, we do the former, namely work in the area where disciplines overlap. This influenced our search terms and the filters we applied in our searches, as described in this chapter. This transdisciplinary approach also influenced our analysis, as each research article we included for analysis contributed knowledge that would not be understood in the same way by a unitary disciplinary lens (Montuori, 2013). The second type of transdisciplinary work mentioned above, namely a collaboration between stakeholder groups, is not part of our study and takes place in real-life contexts outside this book. Our work presented in this volume is designed to make a contribution to such transdisciplinary projects through the tools we developed, in particular a set of questions outlined in Chapter 5 to support real-life struggles for social cohesion in multilingual settings.

Systematic literature review

Our chosen approach to address our research question was a systematic literature review. Unlike other literature reviews which tend to use literature selectively, a systematic literature review aims to include all findable articles that were written about the topic in question. Systematic reviews are used primarily in the health sector but are increasingly employed by researchers in the social sciences to ensure transparency and integrity during the process of searching and screening relevant literature. This section describes how we approached the literature searches in terms of period covered, search terms used, searches and the systematic screening process.

Period 1992–2017

We chose to include articles from 1992 to 2017 for several reasons. For practical reasons, we chose the end of 2017 as the end date, as we developed our search methodology in January 2018 and conducted our searches early that year. Furthermore, opting for a defined period helped us manage the number of articles the searches returned and made the analysis manageable. We chose the beginning of 1992 as our start date for historical reasons, as this was the time when the European Union was established in its current form, the "Iron Curtain" between the East and the West had fallen by then, and what is referred to as the Cold War had ended as a consequence. Around the same time, it was the dawn of the Internet era, which led to new ways of understanding the world and communicating with one another. The period includes the turn of the millennium and its aftermath, which has been defined by increased mobility across national boundaries, and has led to terms such as 'superdiversity' (Vertovec, 2007) to describe societies. Thus, the literature produced during this period is deemed to hold relevance for current times, as multilingualism has increasingly become the norm in many, especially urban, contexts. While we were working on this project, the COVID-19 pandemic took hold of the world, with an impact that is likely to affect the world in many ways, and thus demarcate another turning point in history. This outbreak does not make our project less topical. On the contrary, we observe continued and accentuated societal divisions in our diverse societies and across nations, which makes the topic of social cohesion even more pressing. There is also a data-driven justification. As seen in Figure 3.2, an analysis of article publication dates confirmed that this is a useful period to look at, as the majority of articles concerned with languages and social cohesion were published in the period between 2005 and 2015, and interest seemed to subside in subsequent years. In order to bring the literature up to date, we included additional articles published in the period between 2018 and 2020 in our discussion in Chapter 4; however, they are not contained in the external EndNote Library (Meier, Smala & Lawson, 2021).

Identification of articles

A systematic literature review, such as ours, ensures rigour and quality, by following systematic, transparent and explicit methods. This approach enabled us to identify relevant research literature in peer-reviewed journals from major educational databases (JSTOR, ProQuest and Education Research Complete). We opted for peer-reviewed articles as an accepted criteria of quality research, but we did not include further measures of research evaluation. We included peer-reviewed empirical journal articles (quantitative, qualitative and mixed-method), literature reviews and theory articles (based on evidence), but excluded book chapters, book reviews, comments, speeches, and similar text types that can appear in searches on databases. The methods we employed to identify, screen and assess articles are based on the PRISMA statement (Moher et al., 2009), a protocol specifically designed to guarantee rigour and transparency in systematic literature reviews.

In order to ensure that the searches returned relevant results, we developed an overarching set of keywords drawn from our transdisciplinary framework (Table 2.1) and the literature presented in Chapter 2. The aim of the searches centred on identifying articles that included one or more *social cohesion* keywords, as well as one or more *language* keywords in the full text of the article. The search terms were broad in the first instance in order to cast a wide net and return articles in which explicit as well as implicit links to social cohesion and language were made, or in which a link was made between a particular aspect of language and dimensions of social cohesion. It was critical that the search process uncovered a wide selection of literature and included articles that contained explicit and implicit associations between social cohesion and languages, but we needed to find a "balance between sensitivity (finding as many articles as possible that may be relevant) and specificity (making sure those articles are indeed relevant)" (Siddaway, 2014, p. 2). During the initial stages of the search, it was important to "err on the side of sensitivity" rather than specificity (Siddaway, 2014, p. 2). However, we were aware that "whilst you reduce the risk of missing a relevant item, the number of irrelevant records you have to look through may increase" (Booth, Papaioannou & Sutton, 2012, p. 70). Thus, it was also important to ensure a realistic number of results for analysis.

We piloted a first set of extended keywords and refined the search process to balance sensitivity and specificity. The final search terms included the following social cohesion- and language-related terms:

- *Social cohesion*: social cohesion, community cohesion, intergroup contact, cross cultural (attitudes), social inclusion, social networks, social capital, group cohesion, group belonging, group fragmentation, violence, discrimination, peace, social interaction, stereotype, community relations, identity, power, exclu*, separatis*, extremis*.
- *Language*: bilingual*, multilingual*, plurilingual*, linguistic repertoire, linguistic identity, linguistic capital, language socialization.

The aim of the searches centred on identifying articles that included one or more of the social cohesion keywords, as well as one or more of the language keywords, in the full text. For the final search, terms were combinations of wildcards (indicated above by an asterisk *) and quotation marks (e.g. "social cohesion"), as well as 'Boolean' operators ("AND", "OR"), to search for alternate spellings (e.g. language socialisation or socialization) and variations on a root word. The agreed social cohesion search terms were combined with the language search terms and an appropriate word string was developed, for instance: social cohesion AND bilingual* OR multilingual* OR plurilingual*.

Filters were included to ensure the searches were comprehensive and meaningful, but also manageable. Disciplinary filters: political science, sociology, languages/linguistics, education; Date filter: 1992–2017; Fulltext search; Articles only; All languages (although our search terms were only in English).

As can be seen in Figure 3.1 (PRISMA statement), this search yielded 16,625 articles across all databases. To these, 47 articles were manually added based on previous engagement with the topic. The consequent total of 16,672 records was then screened for duplicates, removing a total of 12,140, including 37 of the 47 manually added, referred to above. This left 4,532 articles, all recorded in an EndNote Library ready for further screening, as described below.

Further screening (reducing data set from 4,532 to 1,812)

As explained earlier, we initially cast the web widely to ensure all relevant articles had a chance to be identified. Even after removing duplicates, we were not able to read 4,532 articles, so we submitted these articles to a round of automatic screening (14 April 2017). For this, we used the smart-group function in EndNote to identify all articles that featured either a social-cohesion-related term or a language-related term in the title, abstracts, keywords or introduction (where no abstracts were available). This was based on the premise that if none of these keywords were mentioned at the beginning of the article, it is unlikely to contain

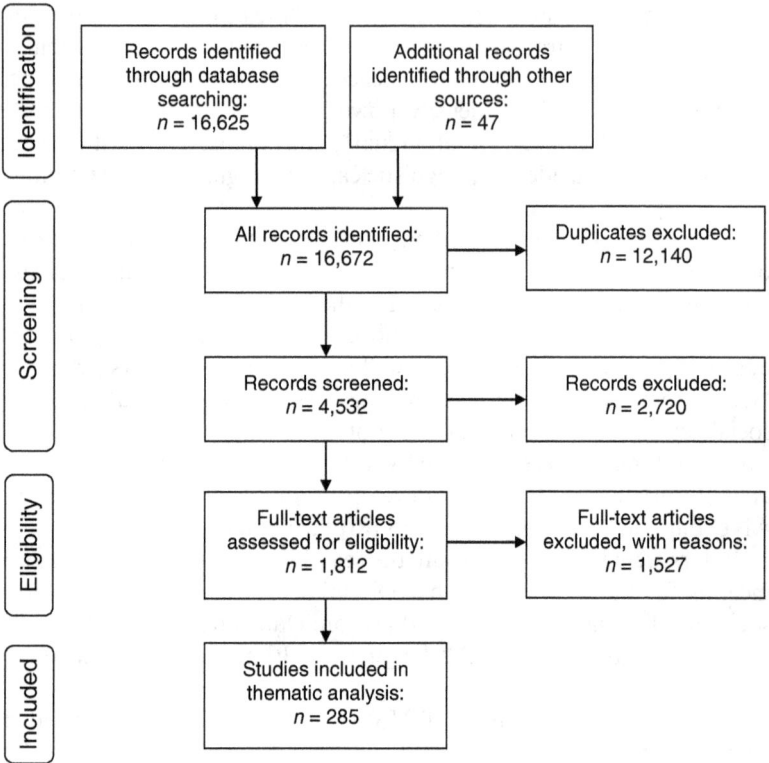

Figure 3.1 Articles identified guided by the PRISMA statement.

relevant evidence. A spot check of 20 excluded articles confirmed this premise. This reduced the dataset to 1,812 articles, ready for full-text inspection by the research team, making the number considerably more manageable and feasible. At the same time, it minimised the risk that some relevant articles may have been overlooked. In the following, we justify the inclusion and exclusion of articles that we included in the final data set that we then analysed.

Articles acceptable for inclusion

As the 1,812 articles had been identified automatically by search engines, we downloaded and opened each of them and looked for explicit evidence that suggested a link between an aspect of language and a social cohesion dimension.

In order to record our inspection results, we exported the bibliographic data of the selected articles (n = 1,812) from EndNote to an Excel spreadsheet and added a number of columns and drop-down multiple-choice menus. These had the aim of (a) identifying relevant evidence: reject or relevant, and (b) recording the reason for rejection where applicable: not an article, no or irrelevant evidence, duplication. Viewing each article, resulted, on the one hand, in 285 articles that contained relevant evidence linking languages and social cohesion dimensions and, on the other hand, in 1,527 articles that were rejected for the following reasons: 1,460 included no relevant evidence, 50 were not peer-reviewed research articles (e.g. book reviews, book chapters) and 17 were further duplications.

Description of the relevant literature

To give an idea of the scope and range of the dataset we generated, we report bibliographic information, including provenance of relevant articles, research design, year of publication and journals in which the articles containing relevant evidence were published, before we report and discuss the results of our thematic analysis in Chapter 4.

Using the search methods described earlier, we identified 285 articles. These were published in the years from 1992 to 2017: an average of 11 articles per year. For 1992 and 1998 none were found, and there is a conspicuous peak in 2011, when the highest number, 35 articles, were published in one year. A column chart shows that the bulk, namely 74% of articles (n = 212) were published in the 11 years from 2005 to 2015 (see Figure 3.2). We might speculate the 9/11 events in 2001 in the USA to be one of the reasons that sparked an interest in social cohesion in different disciplinary fields. It will be interesting to see if the interest in social cohesion and multilingualism/multiculturalism will flourish again following the COVID-19 pandemic.

The research was based on data from 50 countries or regions (see Table 3.1). A relatively high proportion of articles report research that was conducted in countries in which English plays a dominant role: USA (n = 109), UK (n = 23), Canada (n = 16), Australia (n = 10). The remaining 127 studies were from countries with other dominant languages, of which 40 studies used data from more than one country, and 87 articles were from a range of individual countries in Europe, Middle East, Asia, Africa and South America. This means that, despite linguistic and geographical biases, the dataset includes findings from all five continents. In order to portray the global nature of the data, in Chapter 4 we use examples from different countries and contexts to

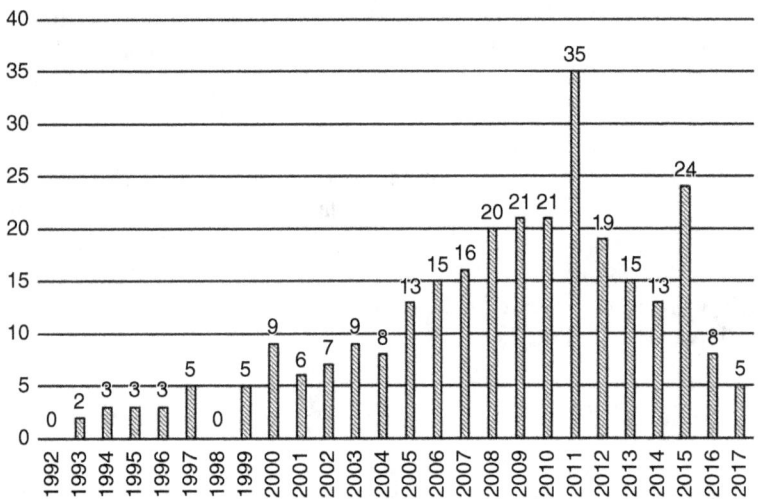

Figure 3.2 Year of publication.

illustrate how links can be made between dimensions of languages and social cohesion in different contexts. Even if a study is conducted in one country, several cultures and language groups often feature, such as in contexts of migration or of minority languages, as language contact manifests itself at individual, group, regional, national and international levels, and of course in the digital sphere. This means we can draw on a wide range of contexts to show possibilities of how languages and dimensions of social cohesion may be linked.

The research methods employed in the 285 articles included 101 qualitative studies, 53 quantitative, 50 theoretical, 38 mixed method, 23 case studies, 8 literature reviews, 3 meta-analyses and 9 practice reports[1] in peer-reviewed journals. The 285 articles were published in 182 different journals as illustrated in Table 3.2.

The journals, as illustrated in Table 3.2, suggest that educational disciplines are clear leaders in the research that links languages and social cohesion, as 116 of the articles were published in a journal with 'education' in the title. Education, as will become evident in Chapter 4, is a particularly salient setting where language and social cohesion concerns overlap. As would be expected in a transdisciplinary literature search based on the search terms we used, additional fields well represented according to the journals titles are sociology/social studies (31 articles), languages/linguistics (30 articles), policy/politics (14 articles).

Table 3.1 Origin of data used in articles

Countries/regions where data were collected	Number of articles per country	Total articles
USA	109	109
UK	23	23
Canada	16	16
Australia	10	10
Israel	8	8
China, South Africa	6 each	12
Singapore, Spain	4 each	8
France, Hong Kong, Ireland, Netherlands	3 each	14
Belgium, Finland, Georgia, Germany, Greece, Hawaii, Japan, New Zealand, Norway, Russia, Sri Lanka, Switzerland	2 each	22
Austria, Bangladesh, Botswana, Bulgaria, Cameroon, Chile, Estonia, Ghana, Hungary, India, Lebanon, Luxemburg, Macedonia, Malaysia, Malta, Mexico, Slovenia, South Korea, Sweden, Taiwan, Thailand, Turkey, Ukraine	1 each	23
International, more than one country	40	40

Thematic analysis

In order to distil the information we needed to answer our research question, we downloaded and read all 285 articles and recorded relevant information in an Excel sheet. We then used this for thematic coding and synthesis. The coding was the joint work of the project team.[2] A team protocol was developed, including frequent team discussions and updates, individual research notes (memos), and keeping a joint code book.

In the Excel sheet, each of the 285 relevant claims was coded under at least one language-related and under one social-cohesion-related code. Guided by relevant methodological work (Saldaña, 2015; Onwuegbuzie & Frels, 2016), we developed a rigorous coding model, as illustrated in Figure 3.3. We developed themes by going through three subsequent cycles. Cycle 1: Free descriptive coding of terms related to language (e.g. minority languages) and to social cohesion (e.g. enabling strong social ties) mentioned in articles that make a connection between languages and social cohesion. Cycle 2: A link was established between language and social-cohesion-related codes, which might be described as pattern

Table 3.2 Journals in which relevant articles were published

Journal name	Number of articles
International Journal of Bilingual Education & Bilingualism	7
Journal of Multilingual and Multicultural Development	7
Anthropology & Education Quarterly	7
Bilingual Research Journal	6
Journal of Latinos and Education	6
Social Science Quarterly	6
International Review of Education	5
International Journal of the Sociology of Language	4
Journal of Peace Education	4
The International Migration Review	4
American Educational Research Journal	3
Compare: A Journal of Comparative Education	3
Ethnicities	3
Journal of Ethnic & Migration Studies	3
Language in Society	3
Mediterranean Journal of Educational Studies	3
School Community Journal	3
Sociology of Education	3
The Modern Language Journal	3
World Englishes	3
Other journals published 1 or 2 articles each	199
Total	285

coding (Saldaña, 2015). Cycle 3: Conceptually related sub-themes, which were informed by the scoping literature in Chapter 2, were bunched or synthesised under overarching themes, which might be described as theoretical or deductive coding, theming the data, or elaborative coding (Onwuegbuzie & Frels, 2016; Saldaña, 2015). In Chapter 4, we will present the literature under these main themes, and unpack this, guided by the sub-themes and free codes developed (see Appendix for full coding structure).

Acknowledgement of bias and limitations

We acknowledge that we operate in an academic world which is heavily biased towards English-language articles published in peer-reviewed journals. Our final set of articles reflected this, insofar as it included only four articles published in a language other than English: one article each in Spanish (Alonso, Durand & Gutiérrez, 2014), German (Meier, 2012a), French (Meier, 2012b) and Portuguese (Ibarra & Calderón,

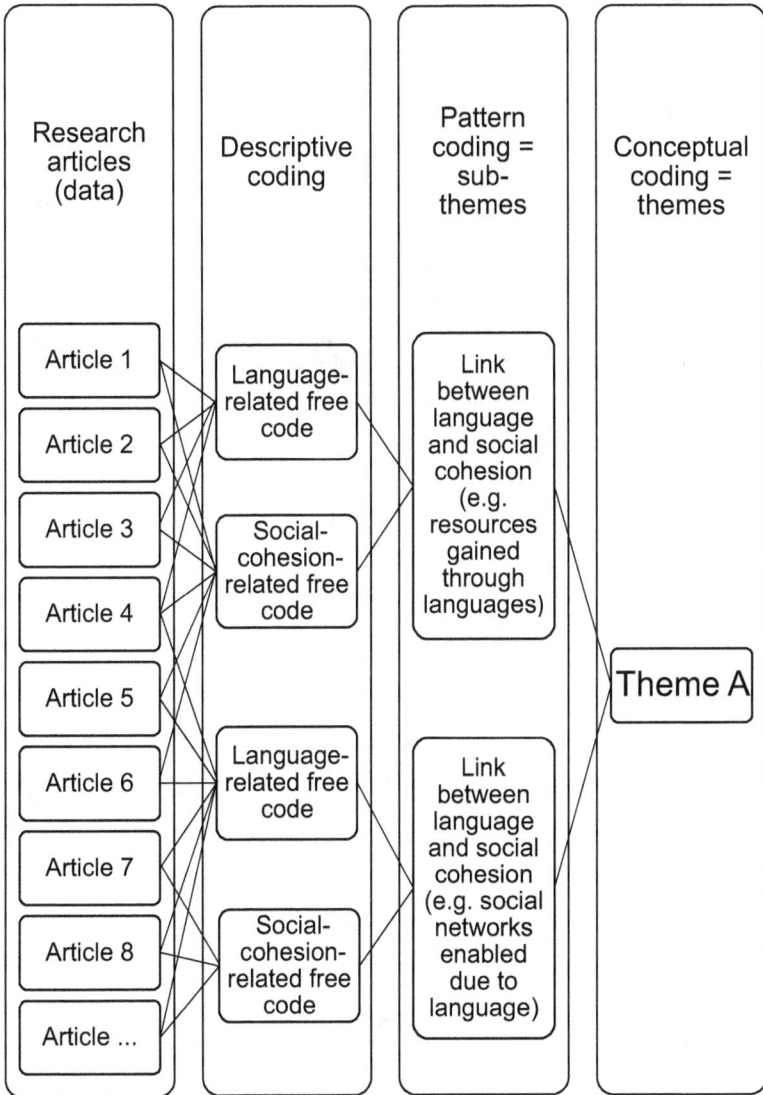

Figure 3.3 Illustration of coding process and development of themes.

2016). (A search in additional languages, and with additional and potentially more context-sensitive search terms, may offer a geographically more balanced insight.)

This means that the findings need to be read with this in mind, and future research is crucially required to address this shortcoming. As described in this chapter, we relied on a rigorous, albeit automatic, search method. The fact that we added 10 articles manually that were not picked up in this way illustrates that no search method is infallible, and there is the possibility that we missed additional articles that might have been relevant. Furthermore, in this book, we treated 'language' as a social tool for verbal, written and signed communication, as defined in Chapter 2, but we did not consider pragmatics, discourse or rhetoric, body language or gesture in our analysis, all aspects of communication which might also be associated with social cohesion. Furthermore, readers should be aware that our research design does not allow us to establish causal or generalizable models, or recipes for individuals or policy makers to follow. What we can show are the types of understandings of the relationship between languages and social cohesion *possible* based on the evidence we viewed, which led us to develop questions that decision makers may want to explore as part of further transdisciplinary collaborative and context-sensitive work.

Notes

1 Practice reports were included, as they offer relevant insights into practical projects that offer qualitative peer-reviewed evidence.
2 The team included, the project leaders (Gabriela Meier and Simone Smala), a research fellow (Helen Lawson) and a volunteer research assistant (Ralph Openshaw).

4 Linking languages and social cohesion

Analysis, themes and examples

This chapter presents the results from our thematic analysis of the 285 articles (1992–2017) selected for our systematic literature review, the methodology of which we described in Chapter 3. The articles included in our analysis feature research findings that link languages with social cohesion in transdisciplinary ways. We crystallised five major themes through data-led (inductive) and theory-led (deductive) coding processes, following Thomas & Harding's (2008) and Saldaña's (2015) key tenets of thematic analysis (see Chapter 3).

Our analysis resulted in five overarching themes, which we present and discuss in this chapter. These themes comprise 14 sub-themes, which in turn include 52 descriptive free codes (see Appendix for a comprehensive list of the themes, sub-themes and codes). The five themes are the following:

a) Social networks and access to resources through languages (languages as social resources that enable interaction, and resources that can be accessed through languages).
b) Norms, attitudes and beliefs related to languages and groups (language assumptions, beliefs and traditions that are often unquestioned).
c) Languages and sense of belonging (desired, resisted, denied or imagined group belonging and positioning based on languages).
d) Manifestations of linguistic behaviour and social cohesion (languages used in different ways to include, exclude and mediate between language and social groups).
e) Language policy and planning and social cohesion (language regulation as a formal social organisation tool).

These themes overlap and interlink in important ways, as illustrated in Chapter 5 (Figure 5.4), but in this chapter we present the themes

DOI: 10.4324/9781003120384-4

separately. Under each heading, we will present a specific way of viewing the relationships between language and social cohesion. Among the research settings that are described in our body of literature, many of the articles investigated social cohesion dimensions in contexts of migration that led to language contact. In addition to migrant and dominant languages present in such settings, the articles described *indigenous* or other *minority* languages, and a small section of literature is dedicated to social interaction opportunities facilitated through learning so-called *foreign* or *modern* languages in general, or English as a *foreign* language in particular.

In the following sections, we will first include a note on how terms and references will be used in this chapter, before we present each theme under five headings. Under each heading, we will then introduce the theme, and relate it to concepts established in Chapter 2, before we provide an overview of the theme, including sub-themes and free descriptive codes. Representative examples and quotes from the articles reviewed will then be used to illustrate themes and sub-themes. At the end of each theme, we compare our findings with the scoping literature from Chapter 2 to help us interpret the insights from our systematic literature review. In order to keep the text readable, we will only present one or two sample articles from our literature review that are representative of the themes and sub-themes. To find further evidence of articles comprised in each of these themes, the reader is invited to access an online Endnote Library (Meier, Smala & Lawson, 2021, https://data.mendeley.com/datasets/ydtms99mjm/3), which contains references to all 285 articles grouped by themes, sub-themes and descriptive free codes.

The structure of the themes, sub-themes and free codes is illustrated in Appendix. As many of the topics we present have been discussed elsewhere, albeit without making the specific links we are making in this book, we complement the body of literature we developed with additional literature from outside our sample of 285 articles and our scoping literature, where appropriate. Combining and integrating literature in this way will help us establish a transdisciplinary synthesis of diverse perspectives that are not normally looked at together. At the end of each theme, we highlight main insights we deem important in the quest to deepen our understanding of the link between languages and social cohesion.

Terms and references used in this chapter

In this chapter, we use concepts connected to languages and social cohesion, as discussed in Chapters 1 and 2. By 'languages' we mean standard, dialect and accented varieties of diverse languages, which are often multiple and layered in individuals, society and groups. While it is impossible to exclude the experiences of individuals when we discuss the articles, our main focus here is on societies and groups. As indicated in Chapter 2, we follow Vetter's (2015) lead and consider language groups not to be fixed, but potentially multiple, fluid and shifting over lifetimes. While we use labels to describe the function or status a language has for the in- or out-groups in the articles we analysed (e.g. *dominant, standard, minority, foreign,* etc.), we urge the reader to view this chapter with the understanding that the use of any such label is not value free, as labels can play a crucial role as an organising principle in societies.

In Chapter 5, we will return to this aspect, as our analysis offers a new conceptualisation of how languages and social cohesion may be linked. In the framework of this, we argue for a conscientious and judicious use of such labels when exploring the language and social cohesion constellation. For this reason, we will print such labels in italics throughout this chapter as an indication that these terms should not be used uncritically.

In this chapter, we will also adopt the concepts of social cohesion as established in Chapter 2. Specifically, we will refer to the dimensions of social networks (largely face to face but also online); linguistic and other resources; norms, values, attitudes and beliefs; as well as sense of belonging and manifestation of behaviour.

To clarify which articles formed part of the body of literature in our sample, we use a superscript 'd' after the brackets – e.g. (Kymlicka, 2011)[d] – to indicate that all references inside the brackets were drawn from our dataset of 285 articles which are included in our online EndNote Library (Meier, Smala & Lawson, 2021, https://data.mendeley.com/datasets/ydtms99mjm/3) and to distinguish them from other literature we use to expand or discuss our themes. In all other chapters of this book, we reference publications in the conventional way without making this distinction.

Theme A: Social networks and access to resources through languages

This theme links several strands of theory, drawing from social capital theorists (Putnam, 2000; Granovetter, 1973, 1983), as well as sociologists of language (Darquennes, 2015; Vetter, 2015; Haarmann, 1990), and other language experts and policy bodies (Council of Europe, 2018, 2001; Busch, 2012; Atkinson, 2011; Lantolf, 2011; Coste et al., 2009).

Theme A is based on 181 articles that focus on how languages can be used to connect within or across linguistic groups, and any resources that are associated with language use.

Our thematic analysis of evidence presented in articles resulted in three sub-themes (social networks and resources, lack of social network and resources, and language competences as a resource). These in turn are based on 14 descriptive codes, as shown in Appendix. In this section, we investigate all three sub-themes together, first describing how languages in their spoken and written form can act as crucial communicative tools that have the *potential* to facilitate social networks and provide access to a variety of resources, before looking at the nature of the ties that can enable access to such resources. The descriptive codes indicate that using *dominant, minority* and *foreign* languages can facilitate weak, strong and multiple social networks which can generate access to resources.

Languages as a social resource

Applied linguists often view languages as a social tool and as a resource that is distributed unevenly in society (Ricento, 2014; Blommaert, 2006). This section confirms that social networks can be built through all available languages, including *minority, migrant, indigenous* or *foreign, modern* and *global* languages, and of course by using *dominant* societal languages.

Language as an essential social resource

We start our report with Grix' (2001)[d] article, which makes the point that languages are a "first stage" or a precondition for successful interaction between groups and for the development of social capital and various types of social networks. The author shows that in the German–Polish border region "respondents with better linguistic skills were able to communicate and interact more freely [across borders], leading to them being far more optimistic on a number of issues than their counterparts who do not share their language abilities" (p. 12)[d]. Languages can, according to this study, open channels of communication and potentially change attitudes, a point we will also explore under Theme B. This aligns with social psychological insights, for instance Branscombe & Baron (2017), who suggest that cooperation across languages can result in positive contact that may influence the way language groups are viewed.

Dominant *languages as a resource*

Dominant language within one polity is often discussed in relation to groups with migrant backgrounds. Not surprisingly, there is convincing and consistent evidence that the ability to use the *dominant* language of a polity or nation is important for social cohesion (Kymlicka, 2011)[d]. This is illustrated by Kostoulas-Makrakis, Karantzola & Athanassiadis's (2006, p. 26)[d] findings from Greece "which show [that] the *majority* language is a strong means of binding together all members of a state, while at the same time excluding those who do not speak it". Indeed, lack of competence in a *majority* language is associated with loss of opportunity for social interaction, among many other disadvantages (Caldas & Cornigans, 2015; Shi, 2011)[d].

Dominant language education for children is often emphasised at school, but adults or parents sometimes lack such opportunities (Yates, 2011)[d]. For instance, some Latin-American populations in the USA have little opportunity to practice their English socially (Worthy & Rodriguez-Galindo, 2006, p. 580)[d]: "Despite valiant efforts, the vast majority do not learn enough to communicate functionally or secure jobs that promise anything beyond simple survival". On the basis of a review of evidence of parental engagement in UK schools, the lack of English proficiency has been identified as a factor in problematic home–school relations (La Placa & Corlyon, 2014)[d].

The above may not be surprising, but these sources confirm that command of the *dominant* language is a social resource that enables parents to support their children's educational aspirations, as well as allows social contact and network building. However, insights into social cohesion are more complex than just knowing the *dominant* societal language well enough to access social resources.

Parent and teacher languages as a resource

In the literature, we generally found much interest in the relationship between schools and the home, and between families and learners. Sturges, Cramer, Harry & Klingner (2005)[d] argued that miscommunication between parents and teachers is common, because of jargon use or because some parents and teachers do not share a common language. The literature uncovered approaches to support vertical home–school relations. For instance Bolívar & Chrispeels (2011)[d] describe a leadership programme for Mexican parents, with children in US schools. This programme was offered in Spanish, which helped parents to build trust with one another, and in the school. This led to a better understanding of the school system, and how parents could get involved. In addition, parents "learning some of the language of schooling [through the course] facilitated the exchange and combination of knowledge among parents and school personnel" (Bolívar & Chrispeels, 2011, p. 31)[d], enabling parent–school social networks based on trust that benefited the parents, the school and the children. Arguably, this programme enabled the school community to collaborate, by opening up bilingual spaces for negotiation and learning.

On the basis of a study of teacher engagement in Canada, it was found that parents' participation in multilingual activities, such as storytelling in school, had the dual effect of engaging parents in the learning community based on their linguistic knowledge, while "increasing appreciation of the children toward their classmates' multilingual abilities" (Guo, 2011, p. 56)[d]. Sturges et al. (2005, p. 97)[d] found that parent–school networks were enabled "when teachers attempted to learn and communicate in the parent's language [...] while the communication itself was not always clear, the meta-message of respect for the language was".

Minority *languages as a resource*

Lopez & Donovan (2009)[d] show that intergenerational communication can be disrupted, for instance through loss of the family language on the part of the children. This can lead to problematic intra-family ties, as communication between children and parents becomes limited. In contrast, intergenerational ties can be strengthened in migrant contexts when parents and children learn the new *dominant* language together, as was the policy in a town in Catalonia (Spain), where the family unit and their migrant language, as well as Catalan (the new *dominant* language in this context), all played a role in the socialisation and integration of learners with migrant backgrounds (Edwards, 2016)[d]. Furthermore, a study with Vietnamese high-school students in the USA (Bankston & Zhou, 1995)[d] came to the conclusion that "literacy in the parental language connects students to a system of ethnic support that can provide encouragement and direction" (p. 15)[d].

Such findings resonate with wider literature that view both system-related, or wider societal, socialisation, and close intergenerational ties, as important features to ensure meaningful socialisation of young people into a new country, as part of close supportive in-group, as well as weak and vertical out-group networks, partly enabled through school (see, for example, Cheong et al., 2007; Coleman, 1988). Command of the *home* language can, therefore, provide social cohesion in the family microsystem, and support engagement with the wider community and their language.

The loss of *minority* languages can negatively affect social relationships within the minority community, as Giuliano (2000)[d] shows. In contrast, *minority* language networks can offer emotional *and* practical support (Amos, 2008)[d]. Amos found that a Japanese ethnic school in the USA helped attendant Japanese students develop their identity, so that they could confidently seek a position in their new American homeland. In this school, nurturing a secure sense of self was found to serve as "a foundation for a successful cultural navigation at a predominantly White school" (Amos, 2008, p. 12)[d]. This suggests that close-tie in-group networks might form a basis to seek the development of weak-tie out-group networks with greater personal confidence and strength, and so may form a foundation for social participation and integration into the new home society. However, we need to be aware that the situation may be different between first-, second- and third-generation groups with migrant backgrounds, as the society they live in may not be new to them. In a newer study, Sall (2020) shows that, for second-generation young people from families with lower-income West African backgrounds in the UK, bilingual resources are important to support their family linguistically, thus bridging between family and wider society. Such linguistic mediation or brokerage for practical reasons may be less necessary in the third generation, and language may take on a different, more symbolic role, in particular with regards to concepts of 'belonging' as will be discussed in Theme C.

Foreign *languages as a resource*

There are some articles with an interest in the learning of *modern foreign* languages. The literature we analysed confirmed Seidlhofer's point (2011) that English is the most studied *modern* language. English is often "embraced for instrumental reasons such as employment, transfer of technology and exchange of information with the broader global community", as demonstrated by a document analysis of policy documents in Singapore by Ng (2012, p. 364)[d], for instance. Thus, English is associated with access to global resources, but not exclusively, as English as a global language can also play a local networking role. For English learners in Malaysia, for instance, the language is used to engage with local internationally minded Malaysian groups, as shown by Shafie, Yaacob & Paramjit Kaur (2015)[d], based on a study of English language students' use of Facebook. Thus, *foreign* languages, especially English, acquired through education, can be used as a resource to connect and expand bridging networks with individuals and groups, both locally and internationally, through face-to-face meetings or digitally enabled contact.

We acknowledge the particular position of English as a coveted resource across many global sites. On the basis of our literature, the role of English as an economic and aspirational global or symbolic *foreign-*language resource is highlighted by Hu in China (2008)[d], and in relation to the problematics of Bangladeshi students attending English-medium schools by Hamid & Jahan (2015)[d]. We return to the role of English under Themes B and C.

A popular way of advancing *foreign* language competences is through stays abroad. In this respect, Jacobone and Moro (2015, p. 318)[d] show that prolonged contact with the target language group through residences abroad can lead to language practice opportunities and the establishment of new intercultural friendships, as well as relationships through the host-families, as could be expected in such international exchanges. In contrast, Shi's (2011)[d] study of Chinese students, who were on short-term residences in the USA, shows that these students had very little, and only superficial, contact with Americans.

Shi (2011), drawing on Bourdieu, argues that language "should be viewed not only as a means of communication but also as a medium for power through which individuals pursue their own interests and display their practical competence" (p. 576)[d]. Shi argues that in the case of these Chinese students, symbolic power, understood as cultural and linguistic capital, was distributed unequally in the American classrooms, which meant that Chinese students had fewer opportunities to speak in class or participate in decision making in group projects. Shi argues that "when functioning in a new community with native speakers, L2 learners with inadequate L2 communicative skills may easily find themselves labelled as incompetent" (2011, p. 576)[d], as was also observed by Blackledge (2001). This means that, on the one hand, the subject knowledge the Chinese students brought to the group was not included in collaborative efforts and, on the other, that these students had limited opportunities to practice their language and improve their communicative resources. These findings resonate with another relevant residence abroad study (Meier & Daniels, 2013), which showed that the most meaningful contacts that led to sustained networks in year-abroad contexts were enabled through making a contribution to society, for instance through volunteering, working or joining a club.

Nature of ties enabled through languages

Social cohesion theorists place great emphasis on weak ties, or networks between different social groups, as crucial for a cohesive society (see, for example, Field 2003; Lin, 2001; Granovetter, 1973, 1983). We found two predominant types of inter-group networks linked to languages in the literature we reviewed: first the ways in which languages can promote relationships between majority and recently arrived migrant groups, and second, home–school relationships (and these often overlap). As shown above, *foreign* languages, including English, may also play a role in building social networks.

Dominant *language is not enough*

Yates' (2011)[d] study illustrates that a shared *majority* language can promote ties between new arrivals and the settled predominantly Anglophone community in the case of recent immigrants to Australia. Her study confirmed that immigrants'

> long-term prospects in Australia depend crucially on the devel-
> opment of links to the Anglophone community in English [...]
> successful interactions in English in early settlement is the corner-
> stone of both the achievement of high levels of English language
> competence and the valued recognition that underpins the mutual
> respect necessary for social inclusion.
>
> (Yates, 2011, p. 457–458)[d]

This important quote indicates that proficiency in the *majority* language not only enables access to local social networks, but that these networks are in turn necessary to develop the language so that fuller access to other opportunities is ensured (see also Shi's (2011)[d] residence abroad study). Yates (2011, p. 458), however, makes the crucial point that "successful interaction in English" might not always be possible despite good or developing language proficiency, as, in her study, many faced "difficulties in reaching out beyond the security of their ethnic bubble to make and develop social connections through English" (p. 469). She concludes that this "signals a problem for social inclusion" (p. 469)[d].

Our analysis of the literature confirms that such findings are not an exception, and that *majority* language competence and a willing-ness to communicate are often not enough to enable successful social interactions or networking (Butorac, 2014; Wright & Bougie, 2007)[d].

Supportive strong-tie networks

The literature reviewed shows that strong-tie networks can be associated with sharing a language (Albirini, 2013)[d], or a language variety or a dialect (Rollock, Gillborn, Vincent & Ball, 2011)[d]. Especially the latter appeared to be associated with trust among fellow speakers (Chong, Guillen & Rios, 2010)[d]. Sharing a language, particularly sharing cultural affinity through understanding the deeper meanings and backgrounds of words and terms (Chong et al., 2010)[d], can establish trusting relationships. The view that a shared language is a mutual source of trust is also part of theories used in social psychology (see Van Lange, Higgins & Kruglanski, 2020, with reference to social representation theory, self-verification theory and shared-reality theory). In refugee situations in New Zealand for instance, bilingual pedagogical activities were able to "build trusting relationships with children and families for those who may have had to abandon trust of authority figures, as part of survival in the refugee experience" (Harvey & Myint, 2014, p. 48)[d]. A shared language or language variety can therefore facilitate close bonds between people, an insight that has been shown by literature on the psychology of group dynamics as well (see, for example, Woo & Giles, 2017).

Exclusive strong-tie networks

Strong-tie networks can also take on an exclusive character (see Field, 2003). For instance, Ibarra and Calderón (2016)[d] describe *minority* language groups in post-colonial contexts who resist engaging with other groups. One particular reason for closing off networks to outside linguistic influences arises when groups perceive their language and culture to be under threat, a phenomenon also observed in the wider literature (see, for example, Hogan-Brun & O'Rourke, 2019). Hermans' (2006)[d] article reports that some groups choose to withdraw into exclusive in-group networks that reject the dominant language and culture, prompted by discriminatory discourses. On the basis of marginalizing experiences, the disregarded linguistic groups, such as Arabic and Berber-speaking Moroccan communities in the Netherlands and Belgium (Hermans, 2006)[d], may then reject civic participation in the wider society.

Other examples indicate similar withdrawal into smaller exclusive strong-tie networks, in which communities and their languages (Levinson, 2007)[d], or language varieties (Beneke & Cheatham, 2015)[d], may be accepted to a greater extent. However, Hermans argues that such countercultures, in which languages can play an important – albeit not the only – role, can lead to "an upward spiral of reciprocal stereotyping and (symbolic) violence which is not conducive to the social cohesion of the societies in question" (2006, p. 99)[d], and may even make young people vulnerable to being groomed by extremist groups.

Multiple networks

Multiple language competences have been associated with resources and networks, specifically through local and translocal ties with diasporic communities (Machado-Casas, 2009)[d], face-to-face and online ties (Shafie et al., 2015)[d], and the simultaneous development of weak and strong ties through speaking *dominant* and *minority* languages (Vedder, Sam & Liebkind, 2007)[d]. In accordance with findings from studies conducted in Catalonia (Edwards, 2016)[d] and New Zealand (Harvey & Myint, 2014)[d], Vedder et al.'s (2007)[d] study from Norway and Sweden illustrates that developing two languages side by side can lead to positive integration and socialisation of young people with immigration backgrounds. The authors found that a good competence level in two languages supported ties with *minority* and *majority* language groups and allowed speakers to access resources from both networks across language groups. This option of developing bilingual skills was not available to the Moroccan participants in Hermans' (2006) study. In their case, an additional perceived lack of respect for their language and culture drove them to develop an exclusive counter-narrative. This can lead to parallel societies (Chan et al., 2006; Field, 2003) which are detrimental to social cohesion.

To expand on the potential networks that are enabled through several languages, we point to Lamarre, Paquette, Kahn & Ambrosi's (2002, p. 47)[d] study of young people's language practices in Montreal (Canada). Interviewees in this study described "their multilingual repertoires as valuable social and symbolic capital, rather like a collection of 'passports' into different social networks, including those within their own ethnic community". Similarly to the Canadian study, Vega, Ang, Rodriguez & Finch (2011)[d] found that bilingual immigrants in Latin-American neighbourhoods in the USA can build strong ingroup ties with Spanish-speaking neighbours as well as out-group ties with English speakers and reap benefits from both.

Insights from Theme A: Linguistic repertoires, social networks and resources

Our thematic analysis confirms, illustrates and illuminates understandings established through research conducted in the field of language-related studies (see, for example, Gerhards, 2014; Ricento, 2014; Atkinson, 2011; Coste et al., 2009; Blommaert, 2006; Bourdieu, 1991). In this field, linguistic repertoires, including languages, language varieties and sociolects, have been viewed as social resources. Language, as a major mode of communication, is understood as a crucial precondition for almost all meaningful social interactions (e.g. Grix, 2001)[d]. The research reviewed illuminates how linguistic repertoires enable people to interact within and between social and linguistic groups, depending on the range and extent of their language competences.

Specifically, our analysis offers evidence that linguistic repertoires can enable a variety of social networks (Albirini, 2013; Hermans, 2006; Vedder et al., 2007; Lamarre et al., 2002)[d], including strong, weak, horizontal and vertical social ties within and across language communities.

Social cohesion literature, as shown in Chapter 2, has established that developing weak ties (ties between otherwise not closely connected groups) are of particular relevance for social cohesion (see Lin, 2001; Granovetter, 1983, 1973), as they constitute the 'glue' that holds potentially quite diverse communities together.

In a multilingual context, a *dominant* language, such as English in the USA, is an important factor that enables social participation according to sociologists (see Cantle, 2006; Chan et al., 2006). Our analysis underpins the understandings that competence in a shared *dominant* language aids the generation of weak ties across diverse communities (e.g. Yates, 2011)[d]. The literature reviewed indicates, however, that in addition to proficiency in a locally *dominant* language (e.g. Yates, 2011)[d], being able to use *foreign* (or potentially *local second*) languages (e.g. Ng, 2012, p. 364)[d] can also support the development of weak social ties with less well-known people across social and linguistic groups locally and globally. Clearly, English occupies a particular place in the hierarchy of languages (Seidlhofer, 2011), and literature on English as transnational linguistic capital (Gerhards, 2014), or on World Englishes, has investigated how new ties are created by learning English (see, for example, Pavlenko & Norton, 2007 or Muza, Lie & Azman, 2012). To this effect, *foreign* languages, including English as one of the lingua francas of our world, have also been shown to serve as tools to build bridging, or weak-tie networks (Jacobone & Moro, 2015; Shafie et al., 2015), which can widen solidarity and collaboration across language and national boundaries (see also Theme C on belonging).

In contrast, strong-tie or bonding networks are based on emotional closeness within groups that share similar characteristics (Cheong et al., 2007; Lin, 2001). Such strong-tie networks can manifest themselves not only as close-knit and supportive groups, but they can also take on exclusive and separatist traits (Field, 2003) that may lead to parallel societies. Our review illuminates how languages can be used for both. In this section, however, we have focussed on literature that illustrates ways in which *minority* language groups in migrant contexts (Amos, 2008)[d], and through dialects, in youth groups for instance (e.g. Rollock et al., 2011)[d], can develop closeness and trust towards members of their shared linguistic *minority* group. It is important to emphasise that such close-tie language networks have been described as conducive to building a sense of belonging and trust within a supportive same-language community. Being a member of such a close-knit in-group gave speakers the confidence to build weak ties to the wider dominant community (e.g. Amos, 2008; Vedder et al., 2007)[d], a point also made by Sall more recently (2020). However, as will be seen under Theme D, close links to a *minority* language group do not guarantee engagement with wider society and may, thus, not lead to weak ties to wider groups (see Shrestha, Wilson & Singh, 2008)[d].

Besides building networks (e.g. Rollock et al., 2011)[d] among members who occupy a similar position in a social and cultural environment in horizontal ways, the language factor has also been found to influence the building of networks vertically (e.g. Bolívar & Chrispeels, 2011)[d], such as between parents and educational institutions. According to Cheong et al. (2007), both horizontal and vertical networks are required to ensure social and civic integration (see also Giardello, 2014), and our review illuminates the role languages can play in this, especially in relation to resources.

Indeed, having access to wider and more diverse networks (strong, weak, horizontal and vertical) means having access to a greater range of resources (Schiefer & van der Noll, 2017). The literature we reviewed demonstrates that linguistic repertoires, as a social resource, can enable access to a range of networks, and through these, access to a range of material, practical and emotional resources that can promote trust and social cohesion (e.g. Ng, 2012; Amos, 2008)[d] locally, nationally, globally and increasingly through digital modes.

Our transdisciplinary reading and analysis of the literature, therefore, established linguistic repertoires – in their entirety – as valuable social resources that can enable multiple, layered and overlapping networks of different strengths, which in turn can enable access to a diverse range of resources. There is an important caveat, however. The following sections make clear that there are complex intervening factors that can complicate, and indeed impede, the translation of this linguistic potential into social networks and resources.

The insights from this theme feed into the framework we present in Chapter 5, insofar as they revealed that the link between languages and social cohesion needs be explored from *distributive* and *behavioural* perspectives. This includes questions around how language repertoires as social resources are distributed in society (distributive), how languages are actively used to build social networks in societies (behavioural) and how access to resources through languages is distributed (distributive) depending on the languages and networks available.

Theme B: Norms related to languages and groups

Theme A summarised that languages – and language repertoires – are a precondition for successful communication that enables access to one or multiple networks, but that language competence alone may not be enough to establish successful social cohesion across groups. In Chapter 2, we have established that social cohesion in and between groups also requires shared ideological values and norms based on a set of ideas (Schiefer & van der Noll, 2017), and a societal language, desires, values and identifications (Bicchieri, 2005). For applied linguists, an examination of language norms reveals expectations of how everyday life should be done (Moore, 2005), including how languages ought to be organised and used in society (Duff & Talmy, 2011). Languages viewed through the lens of language socialisation (Duff & Talmy, 2011; Moore, 2005) can therefore indicate shared understandings and traditions related to languages. Languages can, however, also serve as a proxy for a deeper social problem (Darquennes, 2015; Vetter, 2015) and can be instrumentalised for non-linguistic aims. As will be seen in the following, ideologies that inform language group norms and values might differ, and potentially be the cause of conflict that may limit access to social networks between groups, or enable them.

Theme B therefore presents articles with findings about the interrelationship between ideologies, language use and social cohesion. This theme is based on literature that takes a critical stance on understanding languages and dimensions of social cohesion, often identifying hierarchical constructions of 'superiority' and 'inferiority' of one (language) group over another.

Overall, this theme made use of 111 articles, many concerned with contexts of migration. Evidence is also provided from *indigenous* language and *foreign* language contexts, including English as a *foreign* language. This theme makes visible that norms and attitudes towards languages often have political intentions, or are shaped by such intentions. Theme B consists of just one sub-theme (ideologically informed norms) and seven descriptive free codes (see Appendix).

Attitudinal and ideological dimensions related to languages

We present this theme under two headings. These summarise literature that explores language as a symbolic or indirect factor first, and then as related to an attitudinal or belief system.

Language as an indirect factor related to social cohesion

Having established under Theme A that linguistic repertoires constitute a social resource that enables practical access to diverse social networks and resources, we add here that languages can also take on a symbolic or proxy role. In Chapter 2, we established that views on language use and language groups are influenced by ideologies, defined as a cultural system of ideas that add meaning to an event (Blommaert, 2006; Irvine, 1989), which allows evaluation and is often taken for granted (Riera-Gil, 2019; Gajo, 2014; Ricento, 2014; Blommaert, 2006). Furthermore, issues that seem to be about languages can mask other underlying problems that are not directly related to languages, as outlined by Darquennes (2015) and Vetter (2015) in Chapter 2.

Such insights are confirmed by literature we present in this section (Smirnova & Iliev, 2017; Hamid & Jahan, 2015; de Keere & Elchardus, 2011)[d], insofar as language conflicts can be informed by underlying political differences and identity politics. Smirnova and Iliev argue that language can be politicised "where political views become closely linked to language ideology" (2017, p. 213)[d]. Hamid & Jahan (2015, p. 94)[d] argue that apparent linguistic divides may be "manifestations of the divide that already exists between the two groups who possess differential amounts of capital and exist in different social spaces". Moreover, De Keere & Elchardus (2011)[d] found that personal ideological differences are often the underlying cause of social cohesion issues, rather than different language uses.

Attitudes and beliefs related to languages

Attitudes, being part of a subjective value system, may express intentions that steer behaviour (Chan et al., 2006). Our literature analysis illustrates that groups' positionality towards, or value systems about, languages can be guided by ideologies of assimilationism (Lesar, Čuk & Peček, 2006)[d], monolingualism (Fotovatian, 2015)[d], nationalism (Ovando, 2003)[d], racism (Butorac, 2014)[d], dualistic conceptions of society based on 'us' and 'them' (McAllister, 1997)[d], and discourses related to assumed conflict of civilizations and cultures (Alonso et al., 2014)[d]. Such diverging views can be in conflict with one another in a society and thus hamper socially cohesive societies in the context of multiple language groups. A rejection of language diversity can reveal a nationalist orientation, according to Bourhis, Montaruli, El-Geledi, Harvey & Barrette's (2010)[d] study of students who rejected language diversity and cultural pluralism in a multilingual setting:

> European- and African-American students, in the USA who endorsed assimilationism, segregationism, and exclusionism had a potential for problematic/conflictual relations with immigrants. The psychological profile of such undergraduates showed they had few contacts with Hispanic and Asian immigrants, had unfavorable attitudes toward them, and felt threatened by their presence.
>
> (2010, p. 795)[d]

According to Bourhis et al. (2010)[d], these students, who seem to feel threatened by the presence of other linguistic groups, and strongly identified as Americans and Californians, also endorsed the social dominance ideology, which assumes that some groups are superior to others. Language hierarchies, and superiority narratives, are thus established and upheld. Power can therefore be exerted through languages. Similarly, in Catalonia, the *local official* language of Catalan (considered a co-*official* language in Spain) is viewed as a national symbol associated with social cohesion. Government "resources were specifically allocated to ensure that immigrants had access to Catalan" (Pujolar, 2010, p. 240)[d], as well as Spanish, the *official* language of Spain. However, Catalan might also be a resource some Catalonians are reluctant to share, as there are privileges available through Catalan:

> One can see why many native Catalans may not be particularly interested in the fact that immigrants learn Catalan and thus become capable to compete for the resources and social position that the language gives access to. Again showing that social differences cannot be removed by learning a language.
>
> (Pujolar, 2010, p. 241)[d]

This means that linguistic protectionism may intersect with protecting access to resources and power, and by depriving others from accessing these. Examples such as those from the USA and

Catalonia suggest that if there is competition for opportunities and resources, some people might be reluctant to help language learners keen to master the local language, which could lead to economic strife or even exclusion.

In line with the questionable view that a shared dominant language is enough to promote social cohesion (Butorac, 2014; Wright & Bougie, 2007)[d], monolingual orientations are often constructed as the norm, and a desirable goal in societies, thus implying that other languages and language varieties are not desirable or outside the norm (Hinterman, Markom, Weinhäupl & Üllen, 2014)[d]. In many contexts this is associated with the prioritization of the *dominant* language (Kostoulas-Makrakis et al., 2006)[d], linguistic assimilation (Gast, Okamoto & Feldman, 2017)[d] and indifference to, or promotion of the loss of, other languages (Giuliano, 2000)[d.].

The literature confirms that such monolingual norms are widely held (see Ortega, 2014). For instance, Hinterman et al. (2014)[d] show that a preference for a monolingual society can be found in high school students with and without migrant backgrounds in an Austrian study on student attitudes. Monolingual ideologies can also be expressed through formal monolingual education policies (Arriaza, 2004)[d], and support for remedial school programmes (Kitching, 2010)[d] that have the aim of linguistic assimilation, sometimes prohibiting the use of additional languages (Hermans, 2006[d]; see also Wright, 2004, and Extra & Gorter, 2001).

In the Netherlands, this belief in the *official* languages, to the exclusion of other languages, has led to hardened fronts between majority society who view the Moroccan group's desire to maintain their languages as "proof of not wanting to integrate into society" and the Moroccans who feel their linguistic and cultural background is not respected (Hermans, 2006, p. 92)[d]. The study's findings suggest a suspicion about divided allegiances when *minority* languages are used. However, Hinterman et al.'s (2014, p. 91)[d] study, set in Austria, shows that not all *immigrant* languages are viewed in the same way. Interviewing school students with Austrian and immigrant backgrounds revealed that *immigrant* languages such as Turkish and Eastern/Southern European languages were seen as problematic and disruptive of social cohesion, whereas languages learnt in school, for example English and Spanish, were construed as "necessary and beautiful", and not problematic in relation to social cohesion. This suggests that the teachers and students in these studies equate social cohesion, not only with speaking a *dominant* language, but also with competence in a high-status *foreign* language. Studies, such as these, confirm a monolingual bias (Gajo, 2014; Grosjean, 1982; May, 2014; Ortega, 2014) against at least some *immigrant* languages, indicating that such norms are not only about languages but also about an underlying social hierarchy, as argued by Darquennes (2015).

We also identified evidence of an alternative view, which indicates that some groups accept or welcome the multilingual nature of societies (Baker, 2006). Such orientations are sometimes based on ideologies and attitudes that question "static notions of citizenship, ethnicity, and linguistic identity" (Higgins & Stoker, 2011, p. 410)[d], based on a pluricentric conceptualisation of language (Deffa, 2016)[d], and on the idea of post-nationalism (Kymlicka, 2011)[d]. However, this is a view held within applied linguistics (see, for example, Conteh & Meier, 2014; May, 2014), and in many parts of the world is not really part of a societal consensus, as monolingual norms continue to be widespread and influential (Ortega, 2014; May, 2014; Meier, 2018).

Norms, however, are not static, and projects and policies which validate various (including *immigrant*) languages in schools were identified as a positive force for social cohesion (Kelly 2011; Ratna, Grafton & Macdonald, 2012)[d]. Ratna et al.'s (2012, p. 414)[d] results suggest that embracing "inclusive multiculturalism" in schools by allowing *home* languages to play a role can overcome "barriers across social divides", as well as support *home* language maintenance. This relates to Grix' (2001)[d] study (see Theme A), which suggests that communication and collaboration between linguistic groups can result in positive evaluation of linguistic groups. This seems to be valid in contexts across national borders, as well as within the local context of a school. Literature we viewed also made the important point that so-called linguistic *minority* groups may in fact not be that small. Luke (2003, p. 135)[d] asks, for example:

> how it is that, in countries like the United States, United Kingdom, and Australia (each with over a quarter of their population non-English-speaking in background), literacy and language education continues to routinely categorise the multilingual subject as "Other," as afterthought, exception, anomaly, and "lack".

Multilingual children in schools are thus constructed as outside the norm, as the school system is designed for assumed 'normal' monolingual cohorts. Based on research from the USA (Ovando, 2003)[d], such assumptions can effectively create an 'us' and 'them' based on a perceived ideology of a superior civilization related to the *dominant* or *official* language. Thus, languages as symbolic resources overlap with social legitimacy and status, and what is seen as normal. This means, as de Keere & Elchardus (2011)[d] suggest, that language can be used as an instrument to further ideological aims (see, for example, Duchêne & Heller, 2007; Blommaert & Verschueren, 1998; Kress & Hodge, 1979).

Given that language can act as a proxy for other underlying issues (Darquennes, 2015), Beneke & Cheatham (2015)[d] illustrate how languages and race issues intersect. They found that the use of African-American English (AAE) shaped the attitudes of educators towards this language group – or perhaps it was vice versa? They summarise that "educators' misunderstandings of AAE can unintentionally interfere with children's academic success and sense of belonging as well as result in making inappropriate judgments about children's abilities based on the way they talk" (Beneke & Cheatham, 2015, p. 129)[d].

Unquestioned language norms and attitudes can lead to such stereotyping, especially in education (Donelly et al., 2019), where learners with an accent are often assumed to be less knowledgeable or less intelligent than standard language users (Blackledge, 2001). Some articles in our review found that such forms of stereotyping or 'othering' based on language norms can be internalised by certain groups and can result in negative attitudes about one's own group. For instance, Basford (2010, p. 497)[d] reports that Somali youth in the USA "described feeling fear, shame, and embarrassment to speak their native language and pressure to dress and act in certain ways. [...] resulting in feelings of self-hatred about ethnic origin, cultural heritage, and feelings of being different". This type of internalisation of negative attitudes associated with a group – and their languages – is even more forcefully illustrated by Chen et al. who associate this phenomenon with societal discrimination perceived and internalised by rural migrants to cities in China:

> Some rural migrants have internalized the stigma they experience on a regular basis from urban residents. Migrant respondents identified themselves as inferior and incapable of being on equal standing with residents: We are from the poor rural areas, nobody can change this. We are inferior to urban people because we have limited education, we cannot talk in the standard Beijing dialect, we work on dirty jobs, we wear dirty clothes, and our body is full of offensive smell.
>
> (Chen et al., 2011, p. 28)[d]

This example illustrates how languages and language varieties can contribute to positive or negative stereotypes about societal groups. These stereotypes imposed by self and others can reinforce societal language norms, power structures and ideologies about group hierarchies, and thus can interfere with a sense of social cohesion, inclusion and perceived legitimacy across different groups in society.

Insights from Theme B: Language norms and social power structures

In multilingual societies, norms and beliefs of how languages ought to be organised often trigger debates (Stolle, 2013), as speech communities develop their own social and evaluative language norms (Labov, 1972). Such debates are based on different world views, beliefs and ideologies of how languages should be learned, used and planned for to achieve social cohesion. Such diverging views include, for instance, prioritisation of monolingual societies based on assimilation, coexistence based on maintaining separate language communities, or the idea that socially cohesive societies require meaningful contact between language groups (Stolle, 2013).

Research by colleagues working in sociolinguistics (see Blackledge, 2001; Blommaert, 2006) and language socialisation (for example Ganek et al., 2019; Duff & Talmy, 2011) have been leading the way in interrogating language norms and ideologies that underlie such debates. We also confirmed through our systematic review that language norms and beliefs are informed by ideologies and political contexts (e.g. Smirnova & Iliev, 2017; Kymlicka, 2011; Ovando, 2003)[d], and that languages and associated groups are evaluated differently by different groups (e.g. Gast et al., 2017; Hinterman et al., 2014)[d].

Importantly, language norms reflect and influence power relations in society (Bourhis et al., 2010; Pujolar, 2010)[d] and overlap with other socio-demographic group characteristics (Hamid & Jahan, 2015; De Keere & Elchardus, 2011)[d]. Such findings substantiate the complex and interacting nature of norm-based social relations and linguistic repertoires in multilingual societies. As a corollary, such diverging evaluative views and expectations of how members of diverse language communities ought to behave influence the status languages, language varieties and language communities are afforded.

Our review consolidates the strong arguments (see Donnelly, Barratta & Gamsu, 2019; Lengyel, 2017; Blommaert, 2006) that language norms are often unquestioned and based on popular assumptions, such as those created by monolingual norms (Butorac, 2014; Wright & Bougie, 2007)[d], or the expectation that learning the dominant language suffices to enable social participation (Riera-Gil, 2019; Ricento, 2014). Language norms can, therefore, lead to discourses and rhetoric that position high-status language groups as legitimate, and other language groups as the 'other', effectively creating an 'us' and 'them' based on linguistic categories (e.g. Alonso et al., 2014; McAllister, 1997)[d]. Such positioning of our own and other language groups in wider societal hierarchies, based on language norms and beliefs, may therefore limit social participation, integration and emancipation.

Our transdisciplinary review and analysis of the existing literature firmly establishes language norms and beliefs as highly influential factors in the organisation of a given society. The insight that such norms and beliefs, in turn influenced by historical and political events, are often taken for granted by populations and policy makers is a crucial point that needs to be considered when exploring languages and social cohesion. Norms and beliefs about languages and language groups, alongside norms and beliefs about overlapping demographic characteristics (e.g. ethnicity, religion, socio-economic status), are important subjective factors that determine the extent to which language repertoires can be translated into social networks, resources and belonging (see Themes A and C). Furthermore, norms and beliefs are also an underlying force that influences societal behaviour and policy formulations as presented under Themes D and E.

This theme adds to the framework in Chapter 5, in that taking into consideration the ideological and norm-based – or *ideational* – perspective is important in any exploration of the link between languages and social cohesion. This perspective is closely related to how people feel about belonging to language groups, as we discuss next.

Theme C: Languages and a sense of group belonging

This theme is interlinked and intertwined with studies featured under Themes A and B, namely how a sense of belonging to linguistic groups can be established or negotiated, and what may enable or stand in the way of this. Sense of belonging is a widely accepted dimension of, or indicator for, social cohesion (Schiefer & van der Noll, 2017; Kearns & Forrest, 2000). Applied linguists specifically conceptualises languages and language varieties as a tool for identification (e.g. Norton, 2014; Norton & McKinney, 2011) and belonging to linguistic groups. Such belonging is understood not as static, but as constructed and negotiated, reflecting group dynamics of desired inclusion and exclusion (Fishman & García, 2010). This negotiation of linguistic belonging is shaped by the way other groups think about and treat languages and related groups, the status and power that is associated with each group, and the conclusions groups and individuals draw from this in terms of their own social relationships (Agha, 2007).

Our sample contained 104 articles that pointed towards the interrelationship of languages and sense of belonging. In our analysis, we structured our corpus of articles into two sub-themes, namely evidence about an effective sense of belonging connected to languages and evidence about contested belonging expressed through languages. As shown in Appendix, these sub-themes are based on seven descriptive free codes. In the following, we present and summarise the findings under two headings. First, we report findings related to the types of belonging that are enabled by languages, and then we turn to the way linguistic belonging can be contested and understood as a site of struggle.

Languages and different types of belonging

In the literature we viewed, a shared language is associated with a sense of belonging to linguistic in-groups of *minority* language speakers (Straubhaar, 2013; Machado-Casas, 2009)[d], but also to in-groups of *dominant* language speakers (Yiakoumetti & Mina, 2013)[d], which we will illustrate in this section. A sense of belonging can also occur simultaneously with several linguistic and social groups (Alonso et al., 2014)[d]. Language varieties and accents (Rollock et al., 2011)[d] are also associated with a sense of belonging to an in-group, such as belonging to a professional community, for instance international scientists in Israel (Kheimets & Epstein, 2001)[d]; a religious group, such as immigrants joining a church in Canada (Han, 2011)[d]; or social class, as in the case of working class teenage groups in the UK (Brady, 2015)[d]. In the following we illustrate these points with examples.

Belonging via a shared language

Articles we viewed described how sharing a *majority* language can open doors to feeling welcomed and included, as illustrated in Amit and Bar-Lev's (2015, p. 954)[d] study with immigrants to Israel: "language proficiency [in Hebrew] contributed to a higher sense of national identity and belonging". However, Amit and Bar-Lev (2015, p. 958)[d] add that "it is important to consider the involvement of other migration-related variables including ethnicity".

While proficiency in the *dominant* language can indicate a sense of belonging, the *dominant* language can also be used to delineate nationalist assertions, as evident in examples from Australia (Butorac, 2014)[d], Catalonia in Spain (Kymlicka, 2011)[d], Wales in the UK (Robert, 2009)[d] and the USA (Bourhis et al., 2010). Contextually, these polities are all very different, but the articles cited here all included findings about languages as symbols of nationalism and related belongings. Butorac's (2014, p. 245)[d] study in Australia, for example, showed that learning the *official* language of a country such as English in Australia, and a desire to belong to that nation, is sometimes not enough to develop a sense of belonging or to be accepted into a linguistic and social in-group. This shows that the desire to belong may be in conflict with actual opportunities to belong. Butorac's findings showed that the reality for English learners is indeed more complicated:

> Asian women, even after they had achieved higher than functional competency in English (as defined in the AMEP [Australian Migrant English Program]), they still had to contend with the reality that, when race is a barrier to social inclusion, one's race becomes a defining aspect of the expression of selfhood, albeit an imposed one.
>
> (p. 234)[d]

Findings such as Butorac's (2014)[d] illustrate that people seem to position themselves through the language and language varieties they use, but that the way others perceive them may contest that positioning, as social groups may be judged on criteria other than linguistic.

There is also evidence in our body of literature related to communities displaced by war, prosecution or destitution, including refugees. Deffa's (2016)[d] study looked at linguistic and cultural affiliations of diasporic refugee minorities with Ethiopian (Oromo), Armenian, Pakistani and Somalian backgrounds in the USA and the UK, and found that

> the more homogeneous a group is in terms of language and religion, the more close-knit it will be [...] Consequently, exiled minorities who share the same language and religion are more likely to develop and retain a strong ethnic orientation than groups who are heterogeneous with regard to language and/or religion.
>
> (Deffa, 2016, p. 343)[d]

Close-knit linguistic in-group belonging has the advantage of offering a nurturing and supportive environment but can be exclusive unless such networks are complemented with out-group networks, as suggested by Vega et al. (2011)[d] and Lee, Vera Sanchez and Baba (2013)[d], discussed under Theme D.

Multiple linguistic belonging

Languages are not always used in a fixed or discrete form to signal belonging, or not belonging, as the case may be. In contexts where more than one language is officially used, such as in Hong Kong (Worthy & Rordiguez-Galindo, 2006)[d], Singapore (Alsagoff, 2010)[d] and Catalonia (Kymlicka, 2011)[d], the different languages and code-switching between them can play a role in denoting belonging to affinity groups. In Hong Kong for instance:

> The mixed code has evolved into a complex way of alienating and integrating group members. [...] Results show that the most commonly chosen codes are Cantonese mixed with English, pure Cantonese, pure English, and English mixed with Cantonese. Cantonese is used to ensure understanding, consolidate solidarity and maintain social cohesion.
>
> (Ho, 2008, pp. 10, 15)[d]

Such seemingly deliberate demarcation of group belongings through linguistic codes or varieties was also mentioned with regard to intergenerational interactions. "Teenage" language, in a UK study, was identified as the source of identification for a group that aimed to construct difference between young people and adults and teachers, enabling a sense of belonging and distinction:

> In an attempt to preserve the boundaries of "teenagers" and the "other", many of the adolescents prefer that their non-standard language practices [working class English] should not achieve a status equal to standard English within the classroom. Such a situation would potentially pose a threat to the positioning of the teenagers as a collective, as the apparent linguistic marker of "difference" would be less acute. The majority of the respondents wanted to construct clear boundaries between themselves and "adults", or more specifically "teachers".
>
> (Brady, 2015, p. 156)

This quote hints at the complex group dynamics that can be expressed through language choices. These teenagers may not necessarily reject the *standard* variety, but used language to demarcate age-related belonging while distancing themselves from authority figures. Such behaviour could be seen as limiting to the building of vertical ties, which is a feature of social cohesion (Chan et al., 2006).

Alternatively, learning or using a *standard* language variety can be associated with the desire to belong to the *majority* society, the social class associated with that variety or a region where this is spoken more widely (Yiakoumetti & Mina, 2013)[d]. As an example, Yiakoumetti &

Mina (2013, p. 217) found that teachers in Cypriot schools seemed to use Standard Modern Greek, which "is viewed as the vehicle which allows access to and social inclusion within the dominant social groups" to address the whole class, whereas they used the Cypriot dialect to have informal chats with individual students. This suggests the dual purpose of language use in this classroom to develop formal affiliations to the school system and wider Greek-speaking societies, and to develop informal rapport between people of the same Cypriot origin. The value and status of the *standard* language is illustrated by another study from the UK. This confirms that high-status *standard* varieties of the *dominant* language are important positioning tools at the nexus of class and ethnicity:

> Language and accent were regarded as central tools that enabled black middle class respondents to signal their class status to white others. In these quite sophisticated ways they were able to facilitate the creation of an invisible demarcation between themselves as middle class and other black people from working class backgrounds. [...] "The black middle classes strategically make use of a range of resources including accent, language and comportment to signal their class status to white others to ultimately minimize the effects of racial discrimination".
>
> (Rollock et al., 2011, pp. 1086, 1089)[d]

The examples presented here show that language varieties of various types can be used to express an affinity with age groups, political resistance, territorial unity, systems of authority and formality and social class, as well as building informal rapport.

Another alternative towards new identities is learning *foreign* languages (Shafie et al., 2015; Block, 2007)[d]. Shafie et al. found that learning English in Malaysia enabled learners to imagine belonging to, or identifying as, global citizens through Facebook groups. Specifically females in this study felt a new empowered identity as global English users, as they felt they were not heard in their *native* language, while Block (2007) reports a case where a language learner could thus shed the social stigma of being poor in the new language community. In this way, learning new languages can potentially enable one to escape from social class stigma, or cultural restrictions, and provide access to new networks locally or globally.

There are studies, such as Otsuji & Pennycook (2011)[d], that refer to cases where people with migrant backgrounds feel they belong neither to the language groups of their families nor to that of the local language group, as was the case for a young person with a Turkish background in Australia (Otsuji & Pennycook, 2011)[d]. This person resolved the question of belonging by adopting a new belonging – to Japanese language and culture – based on an interest this student developed autonomously through reading.

The examples offered in this section so far confirm that there is often a tension between the desire to belong and the acceptance of this by the target society or group. This is exemplified by Kelly (2009, p. 5)[d], who argues that emphasising a shared language alone cannot solve such underlying tensions, since "even if people could all understand each other's languages in a technical sense, they would still have a problem understanding each other's identity, culture and sense of being". This is forcefully illustrated by Molinski's social-psychological study (2005)[d], based on a study with Russian job interviewees in the USA. He found, surprisingly, "that high-fluency individuals [of English] were perceived more *negatively* than low-fluency individuals" when they committed an interpersonal or professional faux pas in a job interview (p. 111, original emphasis)[d]. This seems to indicate that humans associate similarity in language proficiency with similarity of norms and behaviour.

Imagined linguistic belonging

In this section, our focus is on imagined belonging, namely how longing to belong can be expressed through language use, how choice or affinity can be connected to an ancestral homeland (Lien, Conway & Wong, 2003)[d] and how speakers of a new language develop a sense of belonging to an imagined community (Kubota, 2011), all in the contexts of globalisation, geographic mobility and migration flows. For instance Lien et al. (2003), writing about communities with Asian backgrounds in the USA, describe "the strong and lingering effect of emotional ties to the country of origin or ancestral homeland. The effective bond is often sustained by adopting ethnic language, religion, food, dress, holidays, customs, values, and beliefs" (p. 469).

While such communities are often looking back in time, other users of languages are looking forward. Kubota (2011) describes how, for learners of English in Japan, "the notion of inclusion is [more] relevant to the desire to socialize with peers and a foreign instructor [of English in Japan] and to belong to an imagined community" (p. 487)[d]. Kubota's findings show that learners of English as a *foreign* language in Japan aspire to belong to a dispersed and "exotic" global group of English users, whose members are not necessarily personally known. Studies like these resonate with work about imagined communities (Anderson, 1983) and the role of languages and language learning (Pavlenko & Norton, 2007) in this, as featured in Chapter 2.

In a study from the USA (Anya, 2011), black students stated as the main reasons to study Spanish or French, that they desired to connect with other black people speaking these languages abroad, thus connecting to an imagined diasporic ethnic group in various locations. Anya found that the learners in her study positively identified "with both classroom communities of learners [concrete] and target language speaker communities [imagined]" (Anya, 2011, p. 459)[d]. Languages, in this example, served as a tool to identify not only with local black groups, but also with a certain imaginary wider group with whom they share ethno-racial affinity, based on a "solidarity among black people" (Student quote, Anya, 2011, p. 456).

The desire to belong to an imagined community derives from an affinity to a wider social group of perceived or imagined "peers". In some cases, this might constitute a favourable precondition for language learning, cross-lingual networking and in all likelihood positive attitudes towards linguistic communities.

Contested linguistic belonging

Language choices might not just reflect a desire to belong to, but can also signal rejection of a community based on context, personal biographies, affinities and imagined future trajectories.

Detachment from local communities

Copp Mökkönen (2013)[d], for instance, shows that immigrant learners in an English immersion school in Finland adopt different ways of integrating linguistically. One student increasingly used Finnish, based on a desire to belong to the local community, whereas another stuck to English on the pragmatic assumption that their stay in Finland was temporary, and Finnish would not be necessary in the imagined future. This decision was informed perhaps by considerations to affiliate with an imagined future rather than engaging linguistically with the local community. Others, also in Finland, linguistically self-segregated due to a strong emotional attachment to a previous phase of their life, which was lived in a different language in a different country (Heikkinen, 2011)[d]. In the cases exemplified in this section, languages are used to affiliate oneself with life in the past or the future, or with international rather than local groups. Such affiliations may generate voluntary detachment from the present location, communities and respective languages.

Threat to one's identity

Articles in our sample also show that language choices can specifically signal rejection of being assimilated and/or fear of losing one's own cultural identity. Thus, social groups may resist the perceived or concrete need to assimilate into larger language groups, or to respond to (perceived) threats against one's language and culture (Rudmin, 2003) by withdrawing into in-groups. Our review includes the example of Chen et al. (2010)[d] describing how Uyghur students in a Han-dominated boarding school chose to use the Uyghur language among themselves to safeguard their identity, and to resist belonging to the dominant culture that is associated with Mandarin Chinese. This is an example of language choices made by minority groups to reject affiliation and assimilation. In many contested regions or post-colonial contexts, language choices are deeply political. In the context of Hong Kong, Chan (2002)[d] describes that English was embraced by local residents to signal that they do not desire to belong to Mainland China, thus using language symbolically to signal belonging to Hong Kong, but not mainland China.

In some cases, communities completely reject other languages, such as the Mapuche in South America (Ibarra & Calderón, 2016)[d], who reject the colonial language of Spanish as incompatible with being a member of their community. In other post-colonial contexts, such as in Africa, "virtually all the former colonies decided to adopt the colonial language – whether English, French, or Portuguese – as the national language and main medium of instruction in education" (Brown, 2011, pp. 196–197)[d]. Brown's study, which looked at the educational policy and ethnic conflict in such contexts, showed that "a denial of mother-tongue educational opportunities can contribute to nationalist backlashes" (p. 196)[d], as "education is a symbolic venue for the recognition of minority cultures, languages, and practices" (p. 202)[d], and thus is a tool that can create linguistic norms of belonging based on assimilation. The feeling of one's own language being threatened by other linguistic groups is often felt by marginalised communities such as "Gypsies"[1] who resist linguistic assimilation into the wider UK society (Levinson, 2007)[d], or by groups migrating within a country to an area where another language is *dominant*, such as through migration from rural to urban contexts in China (Chen et al., 2010)[d]. However, the feeling that one's own language is under threat can also be felt by majority groups, such as by English-speaking Americans in the USA who harbour negative attitudes towards those with other linguistic and cultural backgrounds (Bourhis et al., 2010)[d].

Identity crisis

In some instances, identification with language communities are not possible or not desirable for other reasons. For instance Otsuji & Pennycook (2011)[d] refer to a case where people with migrant backgrounds feel they belong neither to the language groups of their families nor to those of the *dominant* language, for instance the young person with a Turkish background in Australia, mentioned above. This resonates with Hamid and Jahan's findings that Bangladeshi students who attended English-medium education in Bangladesh experienced an identity crisis, as they "were not fully proficient in Bangla, [therefore] they were not true Bangladeshis" (Hamid & Jahan, 2015, p. 86)[d], even though this was their nationality and background. These studies together indicate that linguistic identifications that may be available to some people, be these based on *minority, dominant* or *foreign* languages or on plurilingual situations, may not be available to others, which means that a sense of belonging to groups and the wider society, an important aspect of social cohesion (see Chan et al., 2006; Field, 2003), may be at risk.

Insights from Theme C: Linguistic belonging

Identification with groups and a sense of belonging have been established as a concern of social sciences research (see Schiefer & van der Noll, 2017; Chan et al., 2006) and language-related disciplines (see Norton & Mc Kinney, 2011; Pavlenko & Norton, 2007). Our review work consolidates and illuminates the idea of linguistic belonging as a struggle (e.g. Lavariega Monforti & Sanchez, 2010; Chan, 2002)[d] caught between multilingual realities and diverse personal, social and political agendas.

Our systematic review substantiates that these struggles for identification are complex, layered and nuanced, as explored in our review of conceptual literature in Chapter 2 (see for example Atindogbé & Ebongue, 2019; Sengupta, 2018; Sarroub & Quadros, 2014; Blommaert, 2006; Haarmann, 1990). Language repertoires and a sense of belonging, as a dimension of social cohesion, seem to be strongly intertwined concepts. Our review specifically highlighted the tensions that can occur when a range of layered linguistic and cultural belongings are desired, imagined, contested, resisted or denied.

Linguistic and social/cultural belongings can manifest themselves as narratives of self, for example based on life trajectories (Copp Mökkönen, 2013; Heikkinen, 2011; Lien et al., 2003)[d], and as subjective positioning of self in society (e.g. Hinterman et al., 2014)[d].

Our review strongly supports the argument that language knowledge, and willingness to participate in the social life of a nation, may not be enough to ascertain social participation. For instance, newcomers, when learning the language of a given community might be included in some contexts (e.g. Amit & Bar-Lev, 2015)[d], but they may be rejected in others, for instance arising from nationalist (e.g. Pujolar, 2010)[d] or race-related (e.g. Butorac, 2014; Bourhis et al., 2010)[d] sentiments, based on underlying norms of who can legitimately belong to a group.

An important strand of the literature is concerned with resistance to belong to additional language communities. This is of particular salience in contexts where one's own language community (and/or culture) is regarded as being under perceived or real threat, as can be the case in post-colonial contexts (e.g. Ibarra & Calderón, 2016; Chan, 2002)[d]. The consequence of this can be resistance to – and even withdrawal from – wider societies, which can lead to parallel societies (see Chan et al., 2006; Field, 2003), and pose a problem in terms of social cohesion.

An additional insight relates to the idea that linguistic belonging, as suggested by Pavlenko and Norton (2007) and Anderson (1983), can not only be related to concrete groups of known people, but also to imagined groups of unknown people, for instance to a global group of speakers of a *foreign* language (e.g. Kubota, 2011; Anya, 2011)[d], an ancestral language (Lien et al., 2003)[d] or a national group who use the same language (Kalocsányiová, 2018).

The insights from our transdisciplinary review established linguistic allegiances as a complex affective factor that is shaped by historical and socio-political contexts and prevailing group norms. In addition, linguistic allegiances help people to make sense of who they and others are in a multilingual society, and in the presence of other socio-demographic factors and how they feel about this. This means that language group allegiances are a site of struggle in which tensions can occur between linguistic allegiances that are desired, imagined, contested, resisted or denied. Thus, the language factor interrogated in terms of social cohesion reveals an emotional and subjective dimension which is of great importance for group belonging, not only for individuals but also for groups and wider societies. These insights, which highlight the *emotional* perspective as central to any understanding of the link between languages and social cohesion, are reflected in the framework we present in Chapter 5.

The Themes so far (A, B and C) described the role of language repertoires as social tools to build networks and gain resources, as well as the subjective ideological factors of norms and beliefs that shape the way people feel about their connections to one or more languages and language groups. The next section looks at manifestations of linguistic behaviour that might be viewed as an enactment of language repertoires for social purposes.

Theme D: Manifestation of linguistic behaviour and social cohesion

To understand social cohesion, we also need to look at behavioural manifestations, as argued by Friedkin (2004) and Chan et al. (2006). Thus, our review builds on Chan et al.'s (2006, p. 290) definition of behaviour as an observable component of social cohesion, which comprises "acts of belonging, trust, cooperation and help". The literature we present under this theme is, therefore, about observable social and linguistic behaviours in a setting where several languages and varieties are present. It also builds on the understanding within applied linguists that the way we behave is guided by language ideologies, as languages are enacted before the background of social hierarchies, power relations and social justice issues (Avienieri et al., 2019; May 2014; Ortega, 2014; McIntosh, 2005), language conflict (Darquennes, 2015; Vetter, 2015), mediation and conflict resolution (Schieffelin et al., 1998) and social integration and dissolution (Kalocsányiová, 2018; Stolle, 2013).

As will be shown in the following, languages can be used in separate or integrated ways. Language behaviour has also been shown to bridge between otherwise separate languages. Furthermore, this chapter builds on the idea that language policy and planning in a society has a bottom-up and a top-down component (Nekvapil & Sherman, 2015). Social behaviour, here, is understood as the visible bottom-up enactment or social expression of more subjective language norms, values, power relations, belonging and networks.

Our analysis indicates that 80% (n = 227) of the articles included in our systematic review contained evidence relevant to describing observable behaviour, while they were all coded as part of other themes too. Our analysis yielded five sub-themes that we summarised from 20 descriptive free codes (see Appendix for an overview of the free codes and the sub-themes for Theme D). In the following, we will present these five sub-themes, making visible how linguistic behaviour can relate to dimensions of social networking, norms and values and belonging. To avoid repetition, observations are only included where they can add something additional to previous sections. The sub-themes are summarised under four headings, which relate to languages used to mediate between language groups to establish exclusive networks, as well as to express power relations and belonging.

Mediating between language groups to access networks and resources

We have presented evidence on how languages can act as a social resource to build networks and gain access to resources under Theme A. Here we present an additional strand of literature, which seems of particular relevance to social cohesion, namely that of multilinguals facilitating social networks between other people or groups. Mediation between language groups is a type of linguistic behaviour that has recently received increasing attention in language education studies (e.g. Corbett, 2020; González-Davies, 2020), who view mediation skills as a part of multilingual competences (COE, 2018). Relevant articles from our review include evidence of girls with Latina backgrounds who acted as interpreters in US schools to mediate between parents, students and teachers to smoothen communication (Morales & Hanson, 2005)[d]. Another study offered an insight into children helping parents to manage communication with doctors, authorities and employers (Worthy & Rodriguez-Galindo, 2006)[d], thus enabling access to resources that would otherwise remain out of reach for *minority* language groups.

In this way children take on responsibilities for linguistic mediation, bridging between teachers, learners, parents and authorities. Such mediation behaviour enables inclusion of groups who might otherwise be isolated. There are, of course, two sides to children acting as linguistic brokers. Articles showed that some children took pride in their roles as linguistic mediators and felt important, whereas others found the responsibility, especially of translating for parents in challenging social situations, overwhelming and stressful (Worthy & Rodriguez-Galindo, 2006)[d].

Findings related to languages as tools for mediation are supported by studies on intercultural competence (see for example Cenoz, Gorter & May, 2017; Liddicoat, 2014; Cok & Novak-Kuanovic, 2004) and intercultural citizenship (Guilherme, 2002; Byram et al., 2001) fostered through language education. However, this area of study tends to emphasise individual competences rather than group cohesion and therefore, despite a reasonable inference as to the community level impacts, is not considered further in this book.

Using languages to establish strong (exclusive) in-group networking

Under Themes A and B, we established the role of *minority* languages to generate strong ties and belonging. An important strand in the literature points to the two-sided-nature of *minority* languages for in-groups, as they can be supportive and exclusive at the same time, which can be problematic in terms of social cohesion.

Minority languages and exclusive networking

The literature presented in this section focuses on *minority* languages in contexts of migration and indigenous communities, as their languages not only help maintain links to their cultural origins, which is commonly expected, but they seem to play an important role in supporting populations in unfamiliar environments. Shrestha et al. (2008, p. 143)[d], for instance, describe a concrete example that promoted *minority* language education in an Australian multilingual suburb through informal schooling (also referred to as ethnic or complementary schooling). This venture was shown to generate a non-confrontational and safe environment, promoting "shared social, cultural and linguistic capital" including "bonding capital" that welcomed and included recently arrived immigrants who would otherwise be socially marginalised, and generated "a sense of belonging in their new homeland". However, such supportive endeavours, based on *minority* language use, can at the same time be exclusive, as they can fail to "generate bridging social capital [...] that would enable the formation of interethnic knowledge networks" (Shrestha et al., 2008, p. 143)[d].

Similar findings stem from Inuit populations in Canada (Patrick & Tomiak, 2008)[d], which shows that the Inuktitut language community tends to bond with in-group members for reasons of identification, orientation and support. In this situation, limited English and French competences (the main languages used in Southern cities of Canada) generated hurdles for this group to engage with work and other socio-economic pursuits (Patrick & Tomiak, 2008)[d].

This tension between the exclusive reliance on minority in-group networks and being segregated from the wider society can occur if for some reason opportunities to learn the *dominant* language are not available or accessed, which can result in what some might term ghettoization or parallel societies (Lee et al., 2013; Vega et al., 2011)[d]. This links with wider discourses about multiculturalism (e.g. Modood, 2007; Gutman, 1994) which, however, does not form part of our analytical framework.

Sign-languages and exclusive networking

Sign-language communities are often over-looked in language studies, only two articles were identified in our systematic literature review (Ganek et al., 2019; Obasi, 2008). Deaf communities are described as sharing "a pride in their signed language and cultural norms that are distinct and in some cases in opposition to that of the hearing society" (Obasi, 2008, p. 457)[d]. In this case, being a member of sign-language communities offers a way of emancipation away from the "disability" label, as it establishes a culturally distinct "Deaf identity". This, however, can lead to "exclusion and hurt that has been felt by some people as a result of this quest" (Obasi, 2008, p. 456)[d], as links to out-groups and participation in the wider society are restricted or resisted. Such a reliance on in-group contacts can only be detrimental to social cohesion, as noted in Field's (2003) chapter *A walk on the dark side*.

Norms and power relations related to language use

Under Theme B, we presented articles that link languages with norms and values. This section expands on this, by offering examples that illustrate observable behaviour in which languages and their use are contested, thus influencing social networking and social hierarchies within educational, professional, community and family groups. It also features examples that indicate the role languages play in the positioning of groups within social hierarchies.

Contested norms between linguistic groups

Chávez (2005)[d] introduces a conflict between English-speaking "white residents" and Spanish-speaking families with Mexican backgrounds in a rural town in California. In this context, Mexican parents' involvement in their children's school was constructed by white interviewees at the school as promoting the Spanish language and Mexican culture rather than (white) "Americanness". Chávez (2005, 323–324)[d] argues that this rejection of the Mexican parents' engagement in the school by the "white" parent groups was based on the view that "Mexicans did not subscribe to the white residents' definition of culturally appropriate civic involvement. Thus, they were perceived by white residents as disengaged citizens", and their use of and emphasis on Spanish was seen as evidence for this. This indicates a tension between keeping languages separate and integrating them in the school environment. The rejection of their language meant the residents with Mexican backgrounds felt their language and culture were not respected (Chavez, 2005)[d], which jeopardised collaboration and willingness to do so.

An example from a New Zealand school evidenced a similar conflict, in this case between protecting the *minority* language and culture, on the one hand, and the expectations of inclusion and national unity, on the other (Doerr, 2004)[d]. In this school, the bilingual stream for Māori students was frowned upon by some Pākehā parents (New Zealanders of European descent) who saw the bilingual programme as a dividing force that creates biculturalism and racism in the school. The following quote illustrates that a number of parents (number of interviewees in brackets, out of a total *n* = 68) who enrolled their children in the main-stream programme shared this opinion:

> students did not mix with each other, often having an "us versus them" attitude (21); there were different rules or special treatment of bilingual students (10); bilingual students had a sense of super-iority (6); the bilingual unit encouraged racism/discrimination (4); bilingual students formed ganglike groups (2).
>
> (Doerr, 2004, pp. 240–241)[d]

In contrast, Doerr found that parents from predominantly Māori backgrounds, who have children in the same bilingual stream, did not observe or perceive such divisions. Such findings suggest that more powerful groups might expect inclusion to happen on their terms and in their language, and that in many contexts they are uncom-fortable with minority groups displaying their linguistic and cultural differences, and see this as a sign of social division or lack of willing-ness to adapt. Specifically, Trice's (2004)[d] study from a US university context, unsurprisingly, established that international postgraduates who were more assimilated, namely "students who were culturally similar to Americans, who had minimal language barriers [in English], and who were fairly adept at functioning in the culture were most successful at establishing a social network with their American peers" (2004, p. 684)[d].

Positioning in social hierarchies based on languages

According to our analysis, languages can be used to consciously or unconsciously change social hierarchies in different contexts. For instance, in Deneire's (2008)[d] study of French companies that replaced the working language of French with English, it was observed that con-flict occurred between those employees who found it easier to learn

English and those who found it harder. The less proficient, often older, colleagues thus experienced linguistic and professional insecurity, as they were effectively silenced by the new language regime. This excluded them and their expertise from professional networks they previously belonged to and affected their status within the company hierarchy. In this case, the language change seemed to be the deciding factor.

Studies from other contexts showed that having a high level of a shared language does not necessarily guarantee being included in a professional context either. For instance Fotovatian (2015)[d] found that even with high English competence, English teachers with an accent were marginalised as professionals in Australia:

> The data highlighted how language and accent can turn to tools for othering non-native [English] speakers in everyday community interactions. Lack of knowledge of local discourses and colloquial language contributed to the participants' intense feelings of marginalisation.
>
> (p. 242)[d]

Language aspects, especially pronunciation and accent were instrumentalised in this case to keep existing power structures that seemed to delegitimise non-native speaking English teachers as members of a professional community and excluded them from professional networks. Much literature has confirmed and criticised such norms and beliefs, widely held in the English teaching profession, in which international English teachers are judged on their origin, ethnicity and mother-tongue rather than based on professional qualifications (see e.g. Todd & Pojanapunya, 2009).

Social hierarchies based on languages are also visible in multilingual contexts shared by immigrants of different generations, where bilingualism is foregrounded. Lavariega Monforti & Sanchez (2010)[d] show that division and "internal discrimination" are manifest within Latin-American communities in the USA, which are internally highly diverse in terms of origin and language competence. This study found that, as English is acquired and Spanish lost over time by 1st, 2nd and 3rd generations in bilingual communities with immigrant histories, some groups are stigmatised for losing their Spanish, and others for not speaking English well enough. In this context, this was evident through community internal discrimination and contested and shifting hierarchies, which were marked by competition for resources, such as employment and status within the Latin-American community and in the wider society (Lavariega Monforti & Sanchez, 2010)[d].

Another example of shifting networks, at a more micro level, shows that in the case of recently arrived Latin-American families, family hierarchies can be inverted as young people become more proficient in English than their parents and use less Spanish in the family, thus limiting intergenerational communication (Estrada-Martinez, Padilla, Caldwell & Schulz, 2011)[d], putting family connections at risk. Their study established that this can result in parents losing control over their children, which together with other stress factors, increased the likelihood of young people engaging in risk behaviour, including violent behaviour that resulted in physical, psychological and social injuries (Estrada-Martinez et al., 2011)[d]. This study concludes that supporting the maintenance of the family language, besides English, in education would support intergenerational communication and potentially wellbeing.

Language repertoires used to establish belonging

As established under Theme C, languages are associated with the sense of belonging. Here we expand on this, by showing language behaviour in workplaces and education, and the role that languages and language varieties play in this. A group of articles suggest that languages can be activated together or in layered ways to promote a sense of belonging. This includes flexible language use in a workplace (Otsuji & Pennycook, 2011)[d] and in education (Kelleher & Ryan, 2012; Acker-Hocevar, Cruz-Janzen, Wilson, Schoon & Walker, 2006)[d], as presented in the following with some detail. Integrating languages in social practices have also been referred to as translanguaging (García & Wei, 2014), translingual practice (Canagarajah, 2013) and heteroglossia (Creese & Blackledge, 2014) in the field of language education. Our review offers examples that illustrate how such practices can be related to dimensions of social cohesion.

Integrated language use to demonstrate belonging

Flexible and creative language practices can enable a sense of belonging. Otsuji & Pennycook (2011)[d], for instance, describe a work context in the UK where employees with English- and Turkish-language backgrounds use languages, either "fluidly" mixing, in this case, Japanese and English, or embracing Japanese as an additional language to "claim a new membership and identity by persistently speaking Japanese" (p. 418)[d]. This arguably expresses a desire to belong to a particular social group of work colleagues.

Integration of languages and societies is also the aim in an Albanian-Macedonian bilingual school, where inter-group dialogue was supported by integrating languages in the classroom. In this context, students not only "learn about the subjects of instruction, they also begin to integrate socially and linguistically in the classroom through daily activity" (Kelleher & Ryan, 2012, pp. 83–84)[d]. This Macedonian bilingual project was set up as part of a wider peace effort in multi-ethnic Macedonia, supporting the blurring of boundaries between groups, which might otherwise view one another with suspicion, or may have no contact at all. Kelleher and Ryan describe how integrating two languages into one classroom can foster this aim:

> Teachers tackle lessons of ecology, drama, peace, and tolerance with one teacher beginning a phrase in one language and the other teacher almost seamlessly finishing the thought in the other. By linking the objective of teaching to the objective of peacebuilding, this integrated teaching method creates a shared purpose.
>
> (Kelleher & Ryan, 2012, p. 84)[d]

Language and social integration is normalised in this classroom by the two teachers, each representing a language. They therefore act as role models for language use, in the microcosm of the classroom, modelling meaningful collaboration and mediation between linguistic groups. Such behaviour validates both languages as useful for communication, collaboration and learning and may influence norms associated with languages and language groups. This resonates with wider literature from the field of social psychology, which is concerned with creating meaningful interaction and breaking down segregation (Cantle, 2012; Amin, 2002; Allport, 1954) even though these authors did not specifically consider bilingualism as a conduit for this.

Language varieties used to establish local belongings

Now we turn to diglossic situations where a *standard* language and a local *vernacular* language, or a sociolect spoken by a particular social group, exist side by side in a layered way, as described by Blommaert (2006). As shown under Theme C, language varieties can act as a powerful means of identification. Ender and Straßl (2009, p. 184)[d] found that the Swiss German dialect in Switzerland was used to perform or signal belonging in the case of children with immigrant backgrounds, as they emphasised "aspects of their identities" using their linguistic repertoire. These young people "position themselves as belonging to the ingroup, either of their Swiss friends [using Swiss German dialect] or of their familial and cultural origins [through their family language]". Important to note here is that the *standard* German taught at school played no specific role in building local social networks. There are similar findings from the Veneto region in Italy for example (Goglia & Fincati, 2017), where especially young people strived to acquire the local Veneto dialect, above the Italian *standard* variety, as a means to belong to local friendship circles. Similarly, students in Carter's study in a US high school were acting out "groupness" or "fictive kinship" (p. 322), through expressing their identity and positioning themselves by "speaking black slang, [which was] a commonly shared communication style among these urban minority youth" (Carter, 2006, 315)[d]. The corollary of this is that it is not always the language variety associated with one's own ethnic or cultural group that is used to express the desired local allegiances, but local varieties and sociolects especially play an important role in developing belonging and networks among young people. In Raymond Gann's (2004) study, high-school students with Appalachian [Native American] backgrounds in the USA adopted AAE as this had gained high status among the wider cohort. Raymond Gann's findings resonate with another study on teenage language preferences, namely that by Brady (2015)[d] related to working-class English in the UK, which we mentioned under Theme C.

Thus, participants in such studies enacted and expressed their youth culture through the use of language varieties in a school context. This type of language behaviour does not necessarily signal exclusive belonging, but illustrates the power of languages as a symbol of belonging of their own choosing. Such findings should be taken into consideration in the ongoing debates between advocates of standard German and of Swiss-German dialect use in Kindergartens in the Swiss-German part of Switzerland for instance (Studer, 2006). Blommaert (2006) contends that *standard* and other language varieties are layered in social reality, thus enabling, in theory at least, societal belonging through vernaculars, and at the same time through pragmatic considerations about *standard* language acquisition. These possibilities of multiple belongings through linguistic repertoires need to be carefully considered by policy makers and other decision makers.

Insights from Theme D: Language behaviour

This theme was informed by the argument that objective or manifest behaviours need to be considered in the quest of understanding social cohesion (Chan et al., 2006; Friedkin, 2004). The literature we included under this theme expands such understandings insofar as it reveals how societal use or enactment of language resources, in the presence of language norms and allegiances, can relate to dimensions of social inclusion, social exclusion and mediation between language groups. While there are some overlaps with other themes, important insights in this section stem from the different ways in which languages are used to meet the social needs of linguistic groups, on the one hand, and to reproduce, challenge or transform power-relations and norms in societies, on the other.

Language behaviours can manifest themselves, as groups act to keep languages and language groups apart. Alternatively, language behaviours can integrate two or more languages in every-day lives or social practices. Moreover, bi- and multilingual individuals can use their linguistic repertoires to enable contact between language communities, and thus facilitate connections between otherwise separate language communities.

In considering the above, we start by summarising our insights into behaviours of language separation. The behaviour of keeping languages separate may be adopted in different ways. For instance, newcomers in a society can socialise within exclusive *minority*-language groups, due to limited competence in the locally *dominant* language (Shrestha et al., 2008)[d]. Another way of enacting languages separately is by prioritising one language (variety) over others with the purpose of safeguarding one's culture (Obasi, 2008; Patrick & Tomiak, 2008)[d], or of signalling belonging to a local youth group (Brady, 2015; Ender & Straßl, 2009; Raymond Gann, 2004)[d]. While the former has been observed as potentially leading to separate communities, the latter is not necessarily exclusive, as this foregrounding of one language is context-specific, and may not mean rejection of other groups in other social situations. Prioritising a single (standard) language can, however, also be used to exclude certain social groups from professional spheres (Fotovatian, 2015; Deneire, 2008)[d], or in school communities (Chávez, 2005)[d], by positioning certain languages and social groups as 'others'.

The review of literature also revealed contexts where languages may be integrated or used flexibly, but communities may nevertheless remain separate, or even internally divided. For instance, bilingualism may be foregrounded in immigrant communities as a necessary condition for local belonging (Estrada-Martínez et al., 2011)[d]. In other contexts, such bilingual practices have also been related to the idea of third-culture groups (Dewaele & Oudenhoven, 2009; Kramsch, 2009). This term is based on the idea that members belong neither to one nor to another language group, but constitute a separate bilingual cultural group. Our review indicates that within such bilingual third culture groups, there can also be internal linguistic hierarchies that benefit some groups and disadvantage or exclude others (Estrada-Martínez et al., 2011)[d].

We gained further insights into language behaviours in multilingual settings that integrated language groups in linguistically creative and flexible ways. The behaviour of using mixed codes, or integrating languages in social contexts, has also been described as translanguaging (García & Wei, 2014) or translingual practices (Canagarajah, 2013). These are well-established concepts in the field of language education. In our review, such observable translanguaging behaviour was used to signal (the possibility of) belonging to more than one language community, for instance in education (e.g. Kelleher & Ryan, 2012)[d], as well as in work places (e.g. Otsuji & Pennycook, 2011)[d]. Moreover, role models, such as teachers, who publicly switch between and integrate languages (Kelleher & Ryan, 2012)[d], may be an important factor in shaping language norms, insofar as their behaviour normalises the use of more than one language in spaces in which languages were previously associated with separate communities. Such translanguaging and translingual behaviours that integrate languages flexibly in classrooms have been associated with the creation of inclusive and emancipatory learning environments (García & Sylvan, 2011; Coste et al., 2009; Cummins et al., 2006). Pedagogic considerations of this type are inspired by increasing translingual or plurilingual practices that can be found in multilingual societies (Gajo, 2014).

An additional strand of the literature echoes a recent interest in mediation between languages and language groups as a language education goal (see Corbett, 2020; González-Davies, 2020; COE, 2018). Specifically, our thematic analysis identified bilingual children and young people who bridged between language communities, thus enabling peers, parents and teachers to interact with one another (e.g. Morales & Hanson, 2005; Worthy & Rodriguez-Galindo, 2006)[d]. This type of informal language mediation can facilitate weak networks and social interaction that would otherwise be severely limited or non-existent.

This theme has illustrated that language practices and behaviours can be manifest in separate, multiple, integrated and mediated ways, which may have different purposes and can be exclusive or inclusive, and sought or contested, depending on the situation. The way languages are enacted and used in societies can affect the access to social networks and resources, as well as the sense of belonging to one or more language groups, temporarily or more permanently. Language behaviours and practices can therefore reproduce or transform norms and perceptions of how languages can or should be used, and how language groups are or should be positioned in societies. Insights from this theme, together with those from Theme A, lead us to conclude that the *behavioural* perspective, of how individuals and groups make use of their linguistic repertoires to achieve social and other purposes, needs to be part of the process of understanding the topic under scrutiny in this book. Having looked at the societal language practices and behaviours from a more bottom-up perspective, next we will look at the top-down or formal language policy and planning measures.

Theme E: Formal language planning and social cohesion

In this section, we continue to investigate observable manifestations of language behaviour, but we approach the topic from a formal language policy and planning, or top-down, perspective, as Nekvapil & Sherman (2015) would describe this. Language policy and planning in a given context comprises language status, language acquisition and language corpus planning (Goundar, 2017; Wright, 2004), as explained in Chapter 2. In this chapter we build, above all, on the work by colleagues with an interest in language status planning (Ricento, 2014; NicCraith, 2000; Wright, 2004) and language curricula studies (Reich & Krumm, 2013; Coyle, Holmes & King, 2009), as well as managing language conflict (Darquennes, 2015).

In Theme D, we highlighted research that described particularly pertinent examples of observable behaviour and processes related to the dimensions discussed under Themes A, B and C; specifically, how language use is contested, mediated and brokered in every-day life contexts and any effects this can have on the aspects of social cohesion. Under this Theme (E), we will also cross-over with Themes A, B and C, insofar as we complement them with aspects of formal top-down language planning. This is a crucial aspect, as here the vision for social cohesion and languages is symbolically inscribed and institutionalised, which in turn reflects, influences and steers the development of other dimensions of social cohesion. Thus, there is a close interplay between informal societal (Theme D) and institutional language regulation and planning (Theme E), as argued by Nekvapil & Sherman (2015). Formal language planning is one of the key instruments to organize language acquisition, status and corpus (see Wright, 2004) at governmental level, and language use at institutional or group levels in contexts where multiple languages are present.

Our thematic analysis resulted in three sub-themes, namely language policy, languages in education and types of language education, which in turn consist of 13 sub-codes (see Appendix). Theme E is based on 162 articles, which constitute more than half of the articles we analysed. This means that formal language planning was referred to in many articles in connection with dimensions of social cohesion. A large part of the literature included in this theme focuses on education, as this is where decisions are made that influence the symbolic value of language (language status), and which groups are expected to learn which languages and how (language acquisition). In the following, the three sub-themes are considered together under headings relating to the social cohesion concepts: belonging, norms, social networks and distribution of language resources. In addition, we relate these findings to the large and complex literature on language planning, language management and language change (and other related sociolinguistic fields) as presented in Chapter 2.

Language status planning and a sense of belonging

The examples presented in this section highlight different ways in which language policy and planning can influence belonging at national and group level. Theme B described different types of a "sense of belonging" based on languages. In this section, we add ways in which formal policy decisions may influence linguistic affiliations in different populations groups and contexts.

Post-colonial languages and national belonging

Articles related to linguistic identity politics that aim to unify a nation include examples from post-colonial contexts, such as in Africa and Asia. These illustrate the complexities associated with the adoption of a non-*national* language as an official and/or school language. The official language is often used to teach content in schools, often in the societal presence of many local languages. In Ghana for instance, "many Ghanaians see English as the unifying language and agree that it should be the medium of instruction in schools" (Dei, 2005, p. 240)[d]. Dei argues that this is based on the difficulties that ensue from trying to establish "one local language as the main language, because of a propensity for domination and ensuing resistance". This means that the former colonial language of English, which happens to be a global lingua franca, seems to be widely accepted and plays a positive role in Ghana (Dei, 2005)[d] and in Botswana (Nyati-Saleshando, 2011)[d]. However, the implementation of English as a medium of teaching and learning is not without its challenges, as shown in the following examples.

Hamid & Jahan (2015)[d], also mentioned under Theme C, describe the debate about choosing between Bangla and English as the medium of instruction in Bangladeshi schools. Bangladesh opted to run two systems side-by-side (one teaching content in English and one teaching in Bangla). According to this study, this resulted in "contrastive identities [that] are used to maintain social divisions in global and local terms" (Hamid & Jahan, 2015, p. 77)[d]. In the case of Bangladeshi education policy, they found that the selection of a school medium of instruction alludes to more than a linguistic choice, as "language was used as a proxy for issues of identity and identity politics" (p. 85)[d]. In their article, they argue that the current dual system, distinguished by language of instruction, creates a powerful social divide that "can be traced to British colonial rule, which introduced English to the privileged but denied it to the masses" (Hamid & Jahan, 2015, p. 95)[d]. As shown in Theme C, this system can have implications for identity, not just for Bangla-educated groups, who may miss out on developing a sense of global citizenship, but also for English-educated groups, who may lose their linguistic connection to the nation, while, in addition, it reinforces social hierarchies and power structures (Hamid & Jahan, 2015)[d].

Monolingual conceptualisations of national belonging

The literature features evidence of policy and planning based on monolingual, *dominant* language approaches to steer belonging. This strand illustrates and critiques ways monolingual policies are sometimes promoted as tools to promote socially cohesive societies, for instance in parts of the UK and the USA. According to Gundara (2000, p. 228)[d], "a number of [US] states have declared that they are [English] dominant language-speaking states", with the intention of promoting a local sense of belonging through the English language. This political sentiment is reflected in the 1995 English-only Bill, which Petrovic (1997, p. 246)[d] argues was based "on the presumption that having an official language helps to unify a nation". The article reveals that such policies express the perceived necessity for the one-nation-one-language principle (Wright, 2004). It is important to note that "most language minority parents rate English language learning [in the USA] as one of the most important goals for the education of their children" (p. 249)[d]. However, the article also found that the same people simultaneously attach greater importance to the *minority* languages they use in their daily lives (Petrovic, 1997)[d], based on the strong emotional attachment they have with their languages. This illustrates that a wish to maintain one's own family language is not necessarily in contradiction to wanting to participate in the dominant language society by learning their language. It may, however, explain to some extent the reluctance people might feel to give up one language in favour or another.

This emotional attachment to the familiar language, and reluctance to shift to a new language, seem to become amplified if communities perceive their familiar language to be under threat (see also Levinson, 2007; Hermans, 2006; Ibarra & Calderón, 2016)[d]. Such considerations led Petrovic (1997)[d] to conclude that "erring on the side of democracy and non-coercion by accepting minority language maintenance is ultimately the better choice" (1997, p. 249)[d], compared to banning or prohibiting certain languages in a country or in education. This is based on the argument that perceived linguistic coercion, twinned with lack of respect for community languages, can be met with resistance against the dominant society as shown by Hermans (2006)[d] in the case of Moroccans in Belgium and the Netherlands, mentioned under Themes C and D.

Bilingual conceptualisations of national belonging

In Canada, national belonging was promoted through prioritising the *official* languages of English and French, as shown in a historical overview of language policy in British Columbia (Canada). This study showed that the idea of promoting a bilingual English–French citizenry was seen as a means to "ensure national unity" (Wernicke & Burnot-Trites, 2011, p. 115)[d], based on the two *official* languages in Canada. However, this policy was criticised for ignoring or denigrating the status of other languages in multilingual Canada, and seen as a means to solidify the political and economic power of *dominant* language groups (Wernicke & Burnot-Trites, 2011)[d]. While this policy encourages and supports minority groups to learn French and English and belong to Canada via the *official* languages, it sends the symbolic message that other languages, including Aboriginal languages, or those of recent migration groups, do not belong to Canada, or at least not in an important way.

This means that language status planning efforts, with the aim of creating belonging for, or uniting, all residents, such as in Canada, need to be reconciled with "a world of competing social and linguistic forces, historical and political tensions, and the daily practicalities language teachers and students face in their multilingual and multicultural classrooms" (Wernicke & Burnot-Trites, 2011, p. 124)[d]. The practical argument is an important one, since all language decisions are likely to be a compromise in some ways. However, there have been attempts to be more inclusive of *minority* languages.

Minority *languages and national belonging*

A section of the literature features successful policy efforts designed to promote or raise the status of *minority* languages related to ethnic groups, alongside dominant languages. For instance, Luke (2003) argues that unlike other post-colonial contexts, in New Zealand, *majority* English and *minority* Māori group interests have had a more equal standing, based on the Treaty of Watangi, which was established between the British Crown and Māori chiefs in 1840. Based on its history, Luke argues that, among the countries constructed as monolingual such as the USA, the UK and Australia (in which more than a quarter of the population has a non-English-language background), "New Zealand is a remarkable exception, where all educational and language policy and intervention is responsible for addressing indigenous language and cultural rights" (2003, p. 135)[d]. To illustrate this, Luke (2003)[d] reports that validating *minority* languages beside the *majority* language of English has made the "us" and "them" unstable categories, thus challenging established social and linguistic hierarchies. Such destabilisation, however, does not necessarily mean linguistic and social conflicts disappear.

Around the same time that Luke published his study, Doerr (2004)[d] found that bilingual education, designed to validate Māori, was evaluated differently by Māori and Pākehā communities, as mentioned under Theme D. In addition, other languages associated with recent migration to New Zealand are still subjugated in the linguistic hierarchy and complicate linguistic (and ethnic) belonging for such communities. Cunningham & King (2018, p. 7) found that "participants from most of the language groups mentioned feeling marginalized by New Zealanders". Having shown that language policies, such as those in New Zealand, can create opportunities for an enhanced bilingual sense of belonging, there are other examples from New Zealand and elsewhere that show that this does not offer linguistic identification for all.

Based on a review of how South American countries have interpreted "respect for diversity" in their policy formulations, Beech (2009)[d] uses the example of the 1994 Bolivian Education reform that had the aim to break "with the destruction of indigenous identity" (Beech, 2009, p. 359) and to create a sense of national belonging based on linguistic diversity. Based on this, he illustrates how, responding to a longstanding call by indigenous groups, this reform envisaged every child in Bolivia learning *indigenous* languages in school, regardless of their ethnic and linguistic background (Beech, 2009)[d]. In this case, the aim was to generate bi- or multilingualism as a symbol of belonging and of being Bolivian. However, in this case, the enactment and implementation of such a policy in 1994 Bolivia was hampered by "entrenched racism, sexism, and linguistic discrimination [that] persisted at all levels of the system" (Beech, 2009; p. 359)[d].

This indicates that underlying social grievances and inequalities cannot be addressed through language policy alone, although it may be one component to address such issues. Wernicke & Burnot-Trites (2011)[d], who presented the bilingual policy in Canada, conclude that policies should not simply shift from a *dominant* language focus to a *minority* language focus, but rather adopt a plurilingual approach that enables belonging for all, but they leave it to others to conceptualise such a policy.

Foreign languages and group level belonging

Several articles on foreign language education suggest that language teaching methods may also play a part in language planning to foster belonging, in this case at group level. Here we present articles that look at intensive classroom interaction in a new language – Spanish and French – and how this seems to result in in-group bonding and a strong sense of belonging.

An article from an intensive Spanish project in the USA and an intensive French course in Canada suggests that intensive language learning experiences can result in "social cohesion" (Lynch, Klee & Tedick, 2001)[d], insofar as this resulted in "positive behaviour changes, heightened self-esteem, increased motivation, participation, and engagement" (Joy & Murphy, 2012, p. 103)[d] in the class-room community. Lynch et al. (2001)[d] evaluated a three-month Spanish immersion programme at a US university through which 16 Spanish students studied three social science subjects entirely in Spanish for three months. This programme was found to enable social cohesion in the form of long-lasting friendships within this group based on common interests.

Although, studies like these need to be treated with caution, as findings are often based on self-selected groups, Joy & Murphy's (2012)[d] wider study, including four schools that adopted a five-month three-hour-per-day intensive French programme in Canada, led to similar conclusions. The approach they describe involves "interactive teaching strategies, group work, and an authentic and integrated focus on implicit language learning with [the new] language as a means of communication" (Joy & Murphy, 2012, p. 106)[d]. The enhanced sense of belonging in their study also extended to children with special educational needs. Their study attributes this enhanced sense of group belonging to the nature of foreign-language classes, insofar as they offer a more level playing field (everyone is new and makes mistakes), a common goal (learning and communicating in French) and is "combined with the high levels of social interaction and conversation" (Joy & Murphy, 2012, p. 112)[d] afforded by language studies.

These studies resonate with other authors who suggest that intensive language learning opportunities can result in greater classroom cohesion, specifically increased solidarity and collaboration between peers, as well as sensitivity to their peers' learning needs (Meier, 2014).

Plurilingual conceptualisations and layered belonging

Part of the literature contains studies that link language planning and plurilingual belonging. While Wernicke & Burnot-Trites (2011, p. 123)[d] conceptualise plurilingual competence as a person's "individual cultural capital in a global market", Lamarre et al. (2002)[d] offered an example of what that might mean. They showed that young people in Canada perceived their language repertoires as a resource, namely as a collection of passports as reported under Theme A. This understanding of plurilingualism as a resource is in line with Council of Europe language policy (Council of Europe, 2018; 2014; 2001). See also Maalouf (2008) and Berg & Weis (2007) for plurilingual policy examples from the EU and Luxembourg.

Studies included in our review, such as Phipps &Fassetta (2015)[d] and Kelly (2009)[d], show that a policy approach that foregrounds individual plurilingualism or language repertoires as an educational outcome, and as a normal human condition, may be a way of facilitating concurrent ethnic, national, civic and global belonging, as also found in Lamarre et al.'s study from Canada (2002)[d], where languages denote diverse and overlapping belongings of different strengths for different people. The studies, included here, suggest that validation of diverse languages in education can facilitate and support such multiple and layered belongings. Practically, languages can be validated by making diverse languages visible and audible in schools, for instance through multilingual assemblies, festivals, learning opportunities, team-teaching, library books and by hiring staff representing diverse languages (Acker-Hocevar et al., 2006)[d]. Acker-Hocevar et al.'s (2006, p. 260)[d] study found that, through validation such as this, "respect and trust were reciprocally established between schools and communities".

Language planning and norms and power structures

Adding to Theme B, we focus on language policies and planning efforts that can, on the one hand, underpin power structures shaped by ideological considerations, while, on the other, they can also shape norms, attitudes and beliefs that people associate with languages, with groups who use these and with how they should be used (Duff & Talmy, 2011). In this section, we unpack some of the ideological complexities underlying language policy and planning in multilingual contexts.

Language acquisition planning and diverging ideologies

Policy approaches have been shown to be caught between different belief systems and contested power. Wright and Bougie (2007)[d], for instance, posit that any policy decision related to languages is based on norms, values and attitudes, as illustrated by their study from the USA. They emphasise the controversial nature of language use in education, which is exemplified by California's Proposition 227. This was a successful 1998 referendum that advocated English-only education, by banning bilingual English-Spanish schools. This referendum sparked a fierce debate between opposing factions. On the one hand, there were those who advocated exclusive English-medium instruction in US schools to "benefit minority children by more quickly assimilating them to the dominant language" through English-only instruction (Wright & Bougie, 2007, p. 158)[d]. On the other hand, another faction viewed the English-only movement as involving "institutional practices and policies that undermine the opportunities, status, or well-being of the [Spanish] target language group as a whole" by excluding the first language from learning (p. 158–159)[d].

The English-only movement was based on the belief – or rhetoric – that countries that offer recognition to languages other than the *dominant* or *official* language will in some way fall apart (Petrovic, 1997, p. 232)[d], or that communication will be under threat (Phipps & Fassetta, 2015)[d]. Taking a historical perspective on a similar English-only policy that was adopted in Hawaii in the 1920s and 1930s, Tamura (1993)[d] argues that banning Japanese-English schools had the purpose of reducing the power of Japanese Americans at a time when Japan was seen to be a political threat. Such ideological positions, which are not always informed by research about language learning according to Petrovic (1997)[d] – a point Ricento (2014) also observed – compete for the attention of those policy-makers who are charged with organising educational chances in contexts where people speak several languages.

The difficulty of addressing diverging sensitivities and ideologies in policies is succinctly expressed by Brown (2008)[d], who refers to the delicate nature of language planning in heterogeneous contexts, such as Estonia. In this case, *minority* language campaigners are said to "walk a fine line in their attempts to foster a 'we' identity that promotes regional distinctiveness without being perceived as a threat to national solidarity" (Brown, 2008, p. 8)[d]. Several studies (Phipps & Fassetta, 2015; Wright & Bougie, 2007; Petrovic, 1997)[d] indicate that curricular language choices form part of such larger national and political debates that are related to perceived, potential or real domestic and international threats, as well as hidden ideological agendas (Licona, 2013; Tamura, 1993)[d] and might only superficially relate to children's learning in schools. Thus, the selection of a *national* and educational language, or languages, "embodies and epitomizes the tensions and risks of managing diversity more broadly" (Brown, 2011, p. 196)[d].

Language policies and reconciliation of diverging ideologies

There is some interesting evidence that language decisions adopted within a classroom can moderate ideological divides that may exist in the wider society. According to Davis (2015), the Sri Lankan government aimed to promote national cohesion first through bilingual policies (Sinhala and Tamil), and more recently through trilingual policies (Sinhala, Tamil and English). However, ideological barriers have prevented these policies from taking hold in this "complex and conflict-ridden postcolonial setting" (Davis, 2015, p. 95)[d]. In this context, the national education system "perpetuates the ideology that ethnic groups, as primarily defined by language, are essentially distinct and should be kept separate" (Davis, 2015, p.99)[d].

Davis' research came to the conclusion that the combined use of Sinhalese, Tamil and English, in Tamil as a second language classrooms, "can help destabilize the ideological link between the Tamil language and Tamil ethnic identity by opening up more interactional spaces" (p. 110)[d]. Thus, she recommends integrated linguistic practices, presumably similar to those enacted through bilingual education in Macedonia (Kelleher & Ryan, 2006)[d], and through validation of diverse languages in US schools (Acker-Hocevar et al. 2006)[d], as described above.

Such an approach would mean that several languages are constructed as legitimate resources for learning and collaboration, as well as a symbolic gesture normalising linguistic diversity, based on the underlying aims of wider peace, group cohesion and inclusion. The exposure to, and engagement with, several languages and language groups in the same physical space, thus implemented, may influence hardened norms and attitudes that link language, ethnicity and conflict, at least in some contexts.

Language-sensitive approaches and group cohesion

Some articles suggest that institutional language policies based on language-sensitive or flexible approaches can be conducive to social cohesion. The studies we present here are based on findings from non-governmental organisations. A flexible multilingual policy approach with positive social cohesion outcomes is illustrated by Han (2011)[d], who describes a Mandarin-Chinese Church in Canada, which was attended by a multilingual congregation. This church adopted a language-sensitive multilingual approach that Han associates with successful social inclusion of newcomers. The main points that Han associates with this success are church members' desires to attract others to join a common purpose, in this case practicing Christianity and expanding the gospel. The church thus reached out in different languages to attract members, and helped members practice – and enhance – their English through participation in regular church-related activities in small groups. In effect, this institution welcomed newcomers to Canada in their own languages, as leading members of that church learned their languages, and supported newcomers to use the new language for meaningful inter-action with others. This is in contrast to conventional language courses, in which newcomers are often expected to "learn English as an abstract and discrete linguistic system first, before using it meaningfully for real life purposes" (Han, 2011, p. 390)[d], or where minority language communities may be offered support but remain isolated (Shrestha et al., 2008)[d]. Han feels that other institutions could learn from this example by "allowing or creating opportunities and structuring support for the traditionally marginalized to take on speaking roles within their immediate institutional environment" (p. 395)[d] through the use of several languages.

While religion-led language education initiatives are not uncontested (see e.g. Chao & Kuntz, 2013), the case described by Han (2011)[d] highlights a plurilingual approach to welcoming newcomers and support their arrival in a new society. This example resonates strongly with Acker-Hocevar et al.'s (2006)[d] and Cummins et al.'s (2006) works. The latter reports on newcomers in Canadian classrooms who tell stories about themselves in their first language and flexibly in two languages. A teacher in this study viewed this way of working "not simply [as] a matter of activating students' prior knowledge; it is much more fundamentally fused within a pedagogy of respect" (Cummins et al., 2006, p. 10).

Language planning and contextual circumstances

As shown in previous sections (Themes B and C), languages can be perceived as a threat, and there can be opposition to adopting or promoting certain languages. Phipps & Fassetta (2015)[d] have shown that using policy to change the power and status of additional languages alongside the *dominant* language can bring out fears of a communication breakdown. In their article, the authors specifically referred to the *minority* language of Gaelic in Scotland, which was perceived as a threat to English by some. The authors identified this fear as a "misplaced concern", pointing out that language policy, in their understanding, is not a zero-sum game, in which one language wins and the other one loses.

Carroll and Bebbington (2000)[d] suggest that the success of implementing language policies may depend on popular concerns and local historical circumstances. In Ecuador, for instance, indigenous "demands, when made in the early 1990s, did not appear threatening to a state that still saw its main national security threat as coming from the traditional left" (p. 216)[d]. According to Carroll and Bebbington, this meant that the indigenous movement could develop a strong organisational and networked base without substantial opposition. In this case, Quechua-Spanish (also referred to as Kichwa-Spanish) bilingual intercultural education strengthened the status of indigenous groups and their languages, and enabled them to create strong inter-group networks between indigenous groups. This was evidenced by "a remarkably positive effect on intercommunity cooperation and trust" (Carroll & Bebbington, 2000, p. 443)[d]. This newly gained power was apparently contested later, when the fear of left-wing politics decreased. Awareness and management of such hierarchies of perceived threats and beliefs seem to be a decisive factor in the success or failure of any promotion of social cohesion through changes in language planning.

Language planning and social networks

This section builds on Theme A, which was about how languages can be used as social sources to build networks. Here, we present literature that exemplifies concrete ways through which language policies can enable or hamper opportunities for social interaction between language groups in a given society or across borders. As laid out in Chapter 2, social cohesion is conceptualised, and particularly promoted, through weak ties and multiple ties across different groups (Chan et al., 2006; Schiefer & van der Noll, 20175). This section indicates the role educational language policies in particular can play in promoting or restricting such ties.

Language education to promote weak ties

We identified examples of bilingual schools that were expressly designed as a mission of peace to bridge between communities in conflict, for instance Hebrew-Arabic (Yahya, Bekerman, Sagy & Boag, 2012)[d], as well as a Serbian-Albanian school in Macedonia (Kelleher & Ryan, 2012)[d] mentioned earlier. The Hebrew-Arabic programme Yahya et al. described seemed to exemplify how weak ties between Jewish and Palestinian groups can be developed. This Hebrew-Arabic school was set up specifically to promote "dialog, closeness, and co-existence 'with the other,' both within the Jewish Israeli–Palestinian conflict and outside it" (2012, p. 5)[d]. To the disappointment of some parents, closeness between the communities was hard to achieve. However, weak ties between parents that had not previously existed were indeed enabled (Yahya et al., 2012)[d], as parents who would not otherwise meet entered into conversations. The school could therefore be described as encouraging weak-tie networks to out-groups, which would not exist without this school. Thus, based on some conceptualisations of social cohesion (see Chan et al., 2006), this school seemed to make a positive contribution. Additionally, the school's existence, in itself, may challenge norms or ideologies of how societies should be organised as languages co-exist practically and symbolically.

Structural obstacles to social networking between language groups

Another strand of literature understands systemic or educational structures that segregate linguistic groups as a challenge to social cohesion. Some curricular policies, for example, were found to make networking between groups difficult, by physically separating language groups into different classrooms or school buildings. Similarly to Gomolla and Radtke (2007), who argued that learners with migrant backgrounds are systematically discriminated by the way educational progression is structured, Luna and Revilla's (2013)[d] study, included in our literature review, showed that streaming or tracking in US American schools, when based on academic or linguistic ability, can have negative effects on social cohesion.

According to this study, American students with *migrant* or *minority* language backgrounds are concentrated in lower, less academic, streams, which effectively create a social division, by segregating them from their better performing peers. This might generate a vicious circle of lower achievement, as such segregation limits the opportunities for learners of English to practice and develop the *dominant* language, which is the resource they need (and often want, see Petrovic, 1997)[d] to participate in the wider society. Moreover, it might also limit their opportunities to build social networks across linguistic and socio-economic groups, as well as push young people to socialise in separate groups, which is seen as detrimental to social cohesion. Such educational segregation into different classrooms, based on the language competence, may lead to the kind of parallel societies where communities rely on in-group contacts, as also exemplified by Vega et al. (2011)[d] and Lee et al. (2013)[d] under Theme D.

Furthermore, Langenkamp (2005)[d] found that bilingual schooling in the USA can accentuate physical segregation of language *minority* groups and *majority* learner groups even more, by providing schooling in different neighbourhoods for different language groups. In such situations, children from families with Latin-American backgrounds tend to be concentrated in a bilingual school in one neighbourhood, while students with an English-speaking background are enrolled in the regular school system in a separate school (Langenkamp, 2005)[d]. Some referred to this practice as "hyper-segregation" (Carhill-Poza, 2017)[d]. This was found to be intensified by "white parents' decisions to request transfers" from bilingual school to monolingual English schools, "based on negative views of Latino/a immigrants and bilingual education". According to Prins (2007, p. 297)[d], this trend was exacerbated by the districts' failures to prohibit such transfers. The corollary for Langenkamp is that such structurally enabled divisions create the ordinary (regular schools) and the extraordinary (bilingual schools), constructing an inferior "other" – in this case the "other" being the bilingual school and the students who go there – where less privileged students are concentrated, thus reproducing social hierarchies (Langenkamp, 2005)[d].

Language planning and distribution of linguistic resources

Languages are social resources that are unequally distributed in a society, similarly to other resources (see for example Schiefer & van der Noll, 2017, and a deeper analysis of this phenomenon in Theme A). In this section, we build on Bourdieu (1986) who referred to linguistic capital which can offer social and economic advantages. In addition, literature identified in our sample indicates that language policy and planning choices can re-inforce and perpetuate this unequal distribution, or in turn work towards equalising this.

The distribution of languages as positioning capital

English, being the undisputed lingua franca in the international sphere (Seidlhofer, 2011), is a sought-after linguistic and symbolic resource, which is unequally distributed in the world (Lan, 2011; Hu, 2008)[d]. English is a language enabling global communication, but often it serves as an "economic, social and symbolic capital" sought after by privileged classes (Lan, 2011)[d]. Such arguments resonate with Hu (2008)[d] who critiques English-medium education as a means to reify elite families' privileged position in China (see also Kirkpatrick, 2017; Coleman, 2011 for studies on English medium schools in Asia).

Our literature also included studies on *Foreign* or *modern* languages, other than English, which were similarly found to constitute symbolic and positioning capital in some contexts.

In the literature we reviewed, *foreign* language acquisition planning tends to be associated with resources, rather than other dimensions of social cohesion. As with the view of English as a symbolic resource in the global market, in some English-dominant contexts, such as the UK, *foreign* languages were described as a symbol of distinction, according to Phipps and Fassetta (2015)[d]. Their study from Scotland established that *foreign* language skills in the UK are also unevenly distributed between social classes. They found that increasingly students studying French, German, Spanish and Italian at UK universities are largely from privately schooled privileged backgrounds.

Findings, such as these, imply that there are norms and expectations that learners from privileged backgrounds will need English and other *foreign* languages to build global networks, whereas less privileged learners are expected to rely more on local networks based on the *official national majority* language, and their *family* languages where these are different. Some of these *family* languages are also taught as *foreign* or *heritage* language at school, while others might not be embraced as "valid" for the general school languages curriculum (Cruickshank, Black, Chen, Tsung & Wright, 2020).

Family language choices and the distribution of linguistic resources

One strand of the literature we reviewed considered the element of family choice in their children's language education. We have shown that bilingual education programmes can bring people together (Kelleher & Ryan, 2012; Carroll & Bebbington, 2000)[d] or divide them (Langenkamp, 2005; Prins, 2007)[d], but such efforts can also take an unpredictable path in relation to social cohesion. The literature showed that, in some US schools, middle-class parents tend to remove their children from bilingual education, thus concentrating less privileged English learners in bilingual schools (Langenkamp, 2005; Carhill-Poza, 2017)[d]. Interestingly, some bilingual schools for immigrant groups in Australia (Smala et al., 2013), and particularly in the USA (Valdez, Freire & Delavan, 2016), that were designed to support less privileged groups initially were found to evolve into sought-after symbols of distinction, or positioning capital, for privileged groups who wish their children to achieve linguistic capital (Bourdieu, 1986) or social positioning capital (Smala et al., 2013). This situation has sparked intensive research in the USA where white parents are in some contexts accessing Spanish bilingual programs that were designed as support structures for emerging bilingual Spanish-speaking students (see for example Flores, 2015). Along similar lines, our combined literature indicates that more powerful groups are in a position to choose. They may either embrace (Valdez et al., 2016) or reject (Langenkamp, 2005; Carhill-Poza, 2017)[d] bilingual education, depending on how they evaluate their potential and status.

Flores (2015) frames the struggle around bilingual Spanish-English education in the USA with race-related hegemonies and the reproduction of power relations. Articles from contexts outside the USA in our review reveal that, where parents are given a choice as to in which schools they enrol their children, bilingual education can have the potential to segregate between those who seek to develop two or more languages, and those who may not see the benefit in that (Hu, 2008; Phipps & Fassetta, 2015)[d], or between those who can and cannot afford private bilingual education, if it takes place in fee-paying institutions.

This is exemplified by English-medium school models in China that advantage elites, as illustrated in this quote by Hu (2008, p. 201)[d]: "Rather than foster social cohesion, immersion bilingual programs in China exacerbate social stratification by serving elites that can take advantage of the status, power, prestige, and economic benefits associated with English". Thus, the in-group of such classrooms or schools may be well-bonded, and a sense of belonging may be created through the common goal of learning English, but in terms of the wider society, such programmes can lead to an unequal distribution of linguistic and symbolic positioning capital. Parental or young people's language education choices, where these are available, are likely to be influenced by the norms, values and attitudes they maintain about languages, and the groups who use them. Given family choices are influenced by norms and aspirations, respective language acquisition policies should therefore be explored as one of the reasons why language resources are distributed unequally in society, as observed by Ricento (2014) and Blommaert (2006).

Insights from Theme E: Educational language policy and planning

The literature reviewed under this theme (for example Phipps & Fassetta, 2015; Wright & Bougie, 2007; Brown, 2008)[d] illustrates and strongly supports existing language-focused literature that highlights the controversial, disputed and context-specific nature of language status and acquisition planning (Goundar, 2017; Darquennes, 2015; Wright, 2004) in a given society. Insights from this theme focus largely on the field of education polices and curricula, as these constitute political tools that are used to implement linguistic decisions and norms, and thus influence language status and hierarchies, as well as distribution of languages in a society.

This theme raises awareness that any language decisions and their implementation are delicate processes (e.g. Brown, 2008)[d] that need to take into consideration local debates, ideologies, grievances, aspirations and discourses. Such debates are reflected in the literature, as reports focused on diverging views on *minority* languages and their place in a nation or in an education system, and their status as a perceived threat to social cohesion (e.g. Beech, 2009; Phipps & Fassetta, 2015)[d]. Such debates can polarise societies, as illustrated, for instance, by the much cited debate around bilingual education in the USA (e.g. Wright & Bougie, 2007)[d].

Due to such context-specific debates and sensitives, language planning as a governmental or ministerial concern can have unpredictable consequences. For instance, a bilingual education policy introduced in Bolivia was met with societal resistance that jeopardised the project (Beech, 2009)[d], whereas in Ecuador a similar policy seemed to be successfully implemented (Carroll & Bebbington, 2000)[d]. Reasons for the different outcomes appear to be related to the political climate and the groups that were foregrounded as a threat to cohesion at the time. Such literature confirms the strong influence of contextual circumstances, underlying norms and beliefs and how they influence the interplay between societal language behaviour (bottom-up) and institutional language decisions (top-down), as described by language policy scholars (see for example Nekvapil & Sherman, 2015; Kalocsányiová, 2018).

Educational institutions, as implementers of language decisions, have been associated with the power to either integrate or separate language communities in varied ways. The review established that schools have power to bring together linguistic groups that would not otherwise meet (Kelleher & Ryan, 2012; Yahya et al., 2012)[d], enabling weak and layered networks across language groups. In contrast, educational systems can also structurally segregate groups into different classrooms based on competence in the *dominant* language ability (Luna & Revilla, 2013)[d], thus undermining a sense of togetherness and equality. An additional layer of segregation can occur as schools separate whole groups into different school buildings based on language backgrounds (Langenkamp, 2005)[d], thus adding a geographical dimension to separateness. A further language-based way of separating groups in education is potentially by social class, through offering opt-in *foreign* language programmes (Phipps & Fassetta)[d], that may be taken up by some groups (often high socio-economic), but less so by others.

Foreign language competence, especially English in many Asian countries and beyond, is afforded high status by some families, who use the additional language as positioning capital (Hu, 2008)[d] to gain socio-economic advantages. In situations where such structural separation of groups in education occurs (Vega et al., 2011; Lee et al., 2013)[d] opportunities for social networking across social and linguistic groups in local communities can be limited.

At classroom level, students who find themselves in *foreign* language classes might benefit in other ways, too. Involvement in language learning, in particular through intensive *foreign* language learning projects (see for example Joy & Murphy, 2012; Lynch et al., 2001)[d], can rally student groups together and strengthen the social cohesion in the classroom through intense bonding experiences. This adds to tentative claims (see Meier, 2012a) that intensive language learning may help language learner groups form close bonds.

An additional insight revealed by our thematic analysis concerns the role of respect for language diversity as a way of implementing or shaping language norms. This has been interrogated in the field of language education for some time by scholars focussing on inclusion and equity (see Cummins, 2019; Conteh & Meier, 2014; May, 2014). Our thematic analysis highlights respect for languages also as a policy concern, as this seems to relate to the softening of social hierarchies and enable more egalitarian belonging, at least in schools. For instance, adopting a multilingual school culture (e.g. Acker-Hocevar et al., 2006)[d] was found to have a positive effect on creating mutual respect and trust between language communities. In contrast, lack of respect for *minority* languages has reportedly led to resistance to participate in wider society, for instance on the part of parents who felt their languages and cultures were not respected in school (e.g. Hermans, 2006)[d].

Concluding this theme, our transdisciplinary review of existing literature has confirmed the field of education as one of the main spheres within which authorities can influence language status and hierarchies, as well as dimensions of social cohesion. The literature reports that educational establishments have the power to integrate and segregate language groups, as well as influence the distribution of languages in the population. Furthermore, adopting certain methods of language teaching and learning can influence a sense of inclusion and bonding through respect for linguistic diversity, and through providing intensive language learning opportunities for groups of learners. Importantly, the literature we reviewed reinforces the warning that language policy and planning may not yield expected results, unless societal and contextual sentiments, norms and discourses are carefully considered. Insights from this theme feed into the framework we present in Chapter 5, as they highlight how the way access to language learning is organised in a polity influences the way language resources are distributed in society. This means that *organisational* and *distributive* perspectives make an important contribution to developing an in-depth understanding of the linkages between languages and social cohesion.

As we come to the end of this Chapter 4, we have developed a comprehensive overview of the literature and identified five perspectives (*distributive, ideational, emotional, behavioural and organisational*) from which we can interrogate the topic of this book. An additional perspective that has been identified in all themes, and that necessarily forms part of our framework, as it needs to be included in any such interrogation, is the *contextual* perspective, as the way languages and social cohesion interact is highly context-dependent. Perspectives such the ones we propose were prompted by the social cohesion literature (e.g. Schiefer & van der Noll, 2017; Cheong et al., 2007; Chan et al., 2006; Friedkin, 2004; Kearns & Forrest, 2000); however, in their conceptualisations, languages have not been considered in the multifaceted and nuanced way that we have adopted in this book.

In Chapter 5, we weave the insights from this chapter together into a framework of perspectives that visualises how languages and social cohesion interrelate (Figure 5.4). In addition, our transdisciplinary analysis of themes, presented in this Chapter, underpins a list of questions (Table 4.4) that illustrate possible further explorations into contextually specific linkages between languages and social cohesion, and is designed as a workable set of research starting points. These are designed to support those involved in social cohesion research or decision-making to consider language aspects as issues of importance, which influence the multi-layered dimensions of people's experiences of social cohesiveness or the lack thereof in society.

Note

1 Levinson (2007) deliberately chose this term to describe traditionally nomadic groups in the UK who are referred to as Travellers elsewhere.

5 Transdisciplinary language and social cohesion framework

Tools to support further explorations

In this concluding chapter, we summarise and interpret the results from our transdisciplinary literature review and outline our contribution to knowledge. We expect this to be of relevance in social contexts that seek answers to questions around social cohesion when multiple languages and language varieties are present. The literature that enabled us to develop our insights stems from the following three review stages:

Conceptualisation (stage 1): We started with a scoping literature review (described in Chapter 2) that helped us map relevant fields and define key concepts and dimensions of languages and social cohesion. This guided our systematic literature search, thematic analysis and interpretation.

Identification (stage 2): Following a rigorous search and screening protocol (as described in Chapter 3), we identified 285 peer-reviewed articles (1992–2017 from 50 countries). These articles were subjected to a thematic analysis (described in Chapter 3). Resulting themes, sub-themes and descriptive codes are illustrated in the Appendix. The references of the articles are available online, externally to this book, as a thematically sorted Endnote Library (see EndNote Library, Meier et al., 2021).[1] We consider this library to be an integral part of this book, and as part of our contribution to the transdisciplinary field of the study of languages and social cohesion.

Presentation (stage 3): We presented the results of our thematic analysis in Chapter 4, bringing in some further literature that we deemed relevant in respect to the topics discussed.

The total body of literature accessed (stages 1–3), which we will refer to as the *combined literature* in this chapter, constitutes the foundation of our transdisciplinary literature review, as it occupies the area where several fields of study meet, overlap and share an interest in the

DOI: 10.4324/9781003120384-5

connections between languages and social cohesion (wider applied linguistics, sociology and social psychology, among many others). Accordingly, in this book we do not present new primary research evidence. Instead our contribution consists of summarising, analysing and laying open the interconnected strands of the research that we included during the three review stages.

Guided by our initial research question – *In what way are languages associated with social cohesion in academic articles?* – and the transdisciplinary scoping literature (stage 1), our analytical focus in Chapter 4 was on the interconnections between languages and social cohesion. In brief, Themes A, B and C established the role of language repertoires as social tools that can facilitate social networks and access to resources, as well as the subjective ideological factor of norms and beliefs about languages that shape the way people feel and think about languages, their own language allegiances and those of others, and what they mean in society. Theme D showed how ways of enacting language resources, in the presence of language norms and allegiances, can relate to dimensions of social inclusion, social exclusion and mediation between language groups, whereas Theme E positioned education as an important policy tool which can be used to implement linguistic decisions and norms, and thus steer language status and hierarchies, as well as distribution of languages in a society.

The insights, thus, developed in Chapter 4, led us to the conclusion that the complex interlinkages between language and social cohesion can be understood via six interconnected perspectives, as outlined in this chapter. In the following, we also explain how insights from this book can aid explorations in real-world contexts, where several languages and respective groups are in contact and where tensions might occur. For this purpose, we transformed the insights from our analysis into a series of accessible questions (see Table 5.1 on page 113). These are designed as starting points for further transdisciplinary explorations in which readers from many theoretical and practical stances may want to engage. We go on to add some final words situating this book contextually before, at the end of this chapter, we provide the list of questions for further exploration referred to earlier (Table 5.1).

Transdisciplinary language and social cohesion framework

Based on this large body of hitherto unconnected literature (combined literature), our transdisciplinary language and social cohesion framework, which consists of six perspectives, each containing a series of dimensions, as illustrated in Figure 5.1. Through the preceding chapters we outlined a process which led us, in Chapter 4, to describe the data under five main themes and identify perspectives from which these themes, or aspects of these themes, can be explored. The identification of these perspectives was guided by social cohesion literature we reviewed in stage one (e.g. Schiefer & van der Noll, 2017; Cheong et al., 2007; Chan et al., 2006; Friedkin, 2004; Kearns & Forrest, 2000), and is explained in more detail in the following sections.

We chose to visualise the interconnections between the six perspectives via anintermeshed continuous band that has no start or finish point and features six loops. The loops on the right- and left-hand sides of the figure emphasise the importance of subjective dimensions of social cohesion, which are probably harder to establish and address than the more objective ones. This figure is based on our conclusion that all perspectives are necessary in order to consider how languages and social cohesion interconnect in a given context.

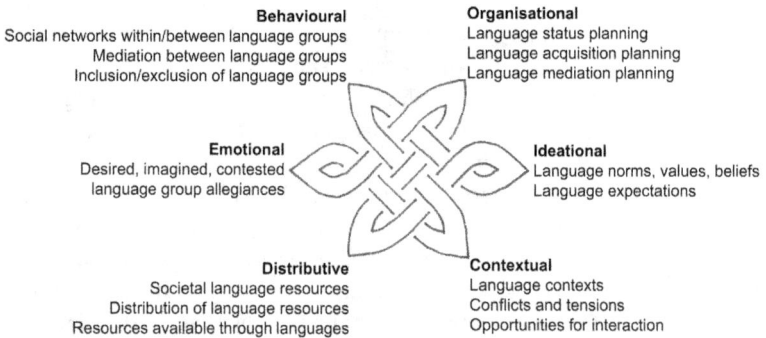

Behavioural
Social networks within/between language groups
Mediation between language groups
Inclusion/exclusion of language groups

Organisational
Language status planning
Language acquisition planning
Language mediation planning

Emotional
Desired, imagined, contested language group allegiances

Ideational
Language norms, values, beliefs
Language expectations

Distributive
Societal language resources
Distribution of language resources
Resources available through languages

Contextual
Language contexts
Conflicts and tensions
Opportunities for interaction

Figure 5.1 Interconnected language and social cohesion perspectives.

Following Chan et al. (2006) we divided the perspectives in this framework into subjective and predominantly invisible (ideational, emotional) and more objective and visible (organisational, distributive, behavioural) perspectives. Some are arguably both subjective and objective (above all contextual and distributive perspectives), as they depend on observable factors such as language laws and the distribution of language resources in a society, on the one hand, and subjective narratives, such as history and societal norms, on the other.

In the preceding chapters, we extensively illustrated and rigorously evidenced how we arrived at the insights and positions we present in this chapter. Here we summarise each perspective, show how each one interlinks with the others and consider future research design considerations related to these that readers might embrace for their own projects. The descriptions of perspectives are expanded by the theory-informed questions contained in Table 5.1, in which we offer concrete examples of how each perspective could be explored.

Contextual perspective

Our review resonates strongly with the argument that social cohesion needs to be understood in its wider sociopolitical context (Green et al., 2006). From the combined literature (e.g. Atindogbé & Ebongue, 2019; Sengupta, 2018; Smirnova & Iliev, 2017; Sarroub & Quadros, 2014; Kymlicka, 2011; Beech, 2009; Pavlenko & Norton, 2007; Ovando, 2003; Carroll & Bebbington, 2000; Haarman, 1990), we conclude that links between languages and social cohesion need to be explored through a contextual perspective, as contextual parameters play an overarching role at societal (micro) as well as at more systemic policy and planning (macro) levels.

Thus, in order to understand how languages and social cohesion interlink, according to our transdisciplinary literature review (see all themes in Chapter 4), we need to establish which languages exist in a given context (e.g. as *official, minority, curricular* and *societal* languages), what conflicts and tensions between language groups may be evident in the past and present, and what opportunities do or do not exist for language groups to meaningfully interact both within and between groups. We envisage this overarching contextual perspective to help understand contextual influences on the ways in which languages and social cohesion dimensions are perceived (subjectively) and enacted (objectively).

In order to establish the contextual perspective, the questions we propose in Table 5.1 are designed to examine historical as well as contemporary factors related to languages, language groups and dimensions of social cohesion, as well as narratives and discourses around these.

Distributive perspective

Access to resources (Putnam, 2000; Granovetter, 1983, 1973), as well as the argument that resources are unequally distributed in society (Schiefer & van der Noll, 2017), forms part of the social cohesion literature. The combined literature (e.g. Phipps & Fassetta, 2015; Ricento, 2014; Smala et al., 2013; Lan, 2011; Hu, 2008; Blommaert, 2006; Bourdieu, 1986) we reviewed evidenced that languages and language repertoires are further valuable social resources (see Theme A), which, like other resources, are unevenly distributed in society (see Theme E in Chapter 4).

The distributive perspective is about establishing the existence and distribution of language resources in a population. This perspective can, therefore, be observed at the societal (micro) level, namely what personal and societal languages exist and what language resources are available in a given population or group. Such linguistic resources in turn can be used to establish both face-to-face and virtual social networks, as described under behavioural perspective. Language resources, thus conceptualised, are typically distributed unequally in societies, as access to learning or utilising *minority, majority, foreign* or other languages varies greatly between people and groups. As languages enable access to knowledge and networks of people, this perspective allows us to explore what other resources may be accessed by population groups within or across language groups, including emotional, practical, economic, social and cultural benefits.

Language repertoires, including varieties, can be established by employing research methods, such as assessment of language competences, visualisations of what languages mean to people and in what social domains they use these, as well as narrative language biographies. To establish the way in which language resources are distributed in a given society requires a correlation of language competences/repertoires with demographic factors, or similar investigations. The questions in Table 5.1 offer a starting point for this.

Ideational perspective

Norms and values in a given population are ideologically informed and an accepted dimension of social cohesion (Schiefer & van der Noll, 2017). Accounts of the ideological or ideational notions of how languages and language groups are evaluated, and how languages should be organised in a society, are well represented in the combined literature we reviewed (e.g. Smirnova & Iliev, 2017; Darquennes, 2015; Ricento, 2014; Wodak, 2012; Blackledge, 2001; Duff & Talmy, 2011; Kymlicka, 2011; Blommaert, 2006; Ovando, 2003). The ideational perspective can be observed at societal (micro) as well as at language policy and planning (macro) level.

The combined literature (see Theme B in Chapter 4) indicates that, in order to explore the link between languages and social cohesion, an awareness is needed of norms. This comprises values and beliefs that underlie perceptions related to how languages are and should be used and learned in a given population, what is expected from different language groups at the societal (micro) level, and popular views of what approach might be most conducive to social cohesion. Such norms are a reflection of power relations and hierarchies in a society and can diverge widely within and across language and social groups. Norms and beliefs about the value of diverse languages guide expectations of why and who is expected to use and acquire which languages, and what this may mean for cohesion in a society.

In order to explore the ideational perspective, which is highly subjective and influences all perspectives, questions, such as those proposed in Table 5.1, could be addressed through ethnographic investigations into narratives and discourses established in different language groups at societal and policy levels.

Emotional perspective

Sense of belonging is a well-established dimension of social cohesion (Schiefer & van der Noll, 2017; Kearns & Forrest, 2000). The literature included in this book firmly makes the link between a sense of belonging and languages and what this can mean for societies (e.g. Atindogbé & Ebongue, 2019; Sengupta, 2018; Ibarra & Calderón, 2016; Sarroub & Quadros, 2014; Norton & McKinney, 2011; Pujolar, 2010; Dörnyei & Ushioda, 2009; Pavlenko & Norton, 2007; Blommaert, 2006; Cummins et al., 2006; Chan, 2002; Blackledge, 2004; Haarman, 1990; Anderson, 1983). Sense of belonging is based on emotions related to languages and language groups; thus, the emotional perspective manifests itself at societal (micro) level and is largely invisible, unless these feelings are translated into action (see behavioural perspective).

Our conclusions, based on the combined literature (see Theme C in Chapter 4), suggest that such sense of belonging or affective group affiliations, based on language, can be dynamic, changing, potentially singular or multiple, complex and layered, and they can be desired, rejected, resisted, imagined or contested, depending on how a person positions themselves and other groups in the world. This perspective shows that language competence and a desire to belong or participate are not enough to access social networks and develop a sense of belonging. Prevailing norms and contextual factors have been shown to steer the types of belonging sought and available in a population. Thus, this perspective firmly posits that linguistic competence is not the sole criterion for successful group affiliations and social integration, albeit a crucial one.

This is a highly subjective perspective that can be explored through the respective questions in Table 5.1, by examining individual and group

narratives and discourses, including biographical accounts of how a
person or a group positions themselves and is positioned by others in a
given population or more widely.

Behavioural perspective

Manifestation of behaviour is described as a visible feature of social
cohesion (Chan et al., 2006; Friedkin, 2004). Relevant literature included
in our book (e.g. Meier, 2018; Schiefer & van der Noll, 2017; Nekvapil
& Sherman, 2015; Gerhards, 2014; Ricento, 2014; Kelleher & Ryan,
2012; Wodak, 2012; García & Sylvan, 2011; Otsuji & Pennycook, 2011;
Clyne, 2008; Kameyama & Meyer, 2007; Blommaert, 2006; Pennycook,
2001; Tollefson, 1991; Bourdieu, 1986) establishes that linguistic behaviour, or social behaviour influenced by languages, can be viewed as the
visible manifestation or enactment of underlying emotions, norms and
language resources. The behavioural perspective is visible and observable at societal (micro) level.

This perspective concerns the social networks people build, based on
their language repertoires, by using one or more languages. It describes
how people use languages to mediate between language groups, and
how people use languages separately or in an integrated way to include
or exclude members or groups related to certain languages and language
varieties. Thus languages are used in diverse ways to negotiate networks,
belonging and positioning in social hierarchies.

According to our combined literature review (see Theme D in
Chapter 4), languages and language repertoires are actively used to
open doors to social networks that enable access to resources. Such
networks can be singular or multiple. Singular strong networks based
on one language or language variety can offer emotional support and
economic, practical and social opportunities, but they may also be
limited in terms of social cohesion if they are not complemented by
weak-tie networks to other language or social out-groups. There is
the possible danger of minority groups becoming insular and exclusive, which under many circumstances can be considered detrimental
to social cohesion in the wider society. However, making use of a language repertoire, including two or more languages and varieties, can be
of benefit not just for minority but also for majority groups, as this can
help bridge and mediate between communities, which may otherwise
remain divided and be seen as the 'other'. Majority language groups
who have no connections to other language groups are not often seen
as problematic in social cohesion texts, but there is an argument that
adding a *foreign* or other language to one's language repertoire enables

new weak networks and a sense of belonging to out-groups that would otherwise remain separate. In consideration of weak-tie networks, our review led us to conclude that the role of translators and language brokers, who can mediate and bridge between language groups, also needs to be considered.

An additional consideration from the combined literature is the symbolic use of language, in that languages can be used in separated or integrated ways, which can reinforce or transform the way languages and language communities are viewed. Using two languages in a space, such as classroom, can, for instance, symbolise togetherness rather than separation.

Developing a concrete (or imagined) sense of belonging to more than one language group has been shown to soften boundaries between 'us' and 'them'. It is important to note, however, that breakdown of relations between language communities often has deeper root causes than linguistic barriers. Lack of proficiency in different languages or language varieties can mask other social malaises or tensions, as language differences often intersect and overlap with demographic factors such as ethnicity, gender, religion, education and economic status. At the same time, observable language behaviour is underpinned by invisible underlying norms and values that influence how social interactions are enacted. In turn, social networks and belonging that language groups establish, or reject and avoid, can steer perceptions by perpetuating or subverting societal language norms and ideational foundations.

Questions related to the exploration of the arguably objective behavioural perspective (see Table 5.1) may require observations of how languages are used to include, exclude and mediate between language groups and negotiate belonging in contexts where languages and language varieties are in contact (e.g. families, groups, communities, schools, companies, etc.). Such research might include observations of sites where interactions take place, or shadowing of people to collect interactional and networking data. Such methods could be complemented with explorations of motivations that underlie manifestation of behaviour.

Organisational perspective

We have established that the complex linkage between language policy and planning and the organisation of language in society is not typically considered in social cohesion research. However, our combined literature reviewed (e.g. Goundar, 2017; Phipps & Fassetta, 2015; Darquennes, 2015; Nekvapil & Sherman, 2015; Vetter, 2015; Ricento,

2014; Wright & Bougie, 2007; Brown, 2008; Wright, 2004; NicCraith, 2000) strongly suggests that this perspective is of great importance in understanding social cohesion in society. Our interpretation is guided by literature on language status and acquisition planning (see, e.g., Wright, 2004; NicCraith, 2000). Overall, the organisational perspective can be observed at the language policy and planning (macro) level: states, organisations, institutions, companies, families and other groups can formulate language rules to organise language use and distribution and influence the status of a language within their spheres of influence. Similarly to the behavioural perspective, languages as viewed from the organisational perspective overlap with other socio-demographic characteristics. Thus, what is presented as a language policy can also be related to other underlying sociopolitical issues.

From our combined literature review (see Theme E in Chapter 4), we conclude that language rules and planning efforts are objective insofar as they can be visible, observable or audible. Such observable rules, laws and policy directives are inscribed in legal and other documents, or agreed verbally in groups. Decision makers can influence language status and use, above all at state level, through adopting official languages and recognising, or marginalising, other languages such as *minority*, *indigenous* or *foreign* languages. In addition, states have a powerful policy tool at their disposal – education – through which language learning and use can be steered, influenced or enforced through language acquisition and status planning.

Languages adopted for teaching and learning, as well as access to language learning provision inscribed in curricula, have great power to steer the status of languages, and that of the groups who speak or are learning these languages. Curricula also steer the distribution of languages in society, which has the effect of influencing linguistic and social hierarchies in a society by raising or acknowledging the status of some but not other languages. Language rules and regulations are an observable expression or manifestation of how linguistic resources are intended to be distributed in the population and hence what social networks and affiliations within and between language groups are envisaged by those with decision power.

The status formally accorded to a language, or to several languages, has an effect on how subjective perceptions and norms are formed. A laissez-faire approach, where language use and learning is not regulated, is a language planning decision in its own right, which might suggest that the status quo of prevailing norms is acceptable to decision makers and members of the dominant language group.

In addition, language mediation planning is about making provisions that allow language brokers to facilitate social networks between language groups that would not exist without them. This is an aspect related to social cohesion that has been largely omitted as a research focus to date.

In order to approach the link between languages and social cohesion from the organisational perspective, we need to explore questions, such as those included in Table 5.1, that relate to language status planning, language acquisition planning and an additional dimension, namely language mediation planning. This perspective can be approached by examining language planning documents, including policies, curricula, mission statements, as well as non-verbal agreements, made at different levels of language policy and planning processes, and by how they are perceived by groups who are affected by them.

Translating our framework of perspectives into practice

Transdisciplinary work consists of two layers. On the one hand, it is about working in the space where academic disciplines overlap and, on the other, it is about bringing together researchers and stakeholders to make practical sense of a topic (Montuori, 2013). In this book, we have addressed the former by bringing together and analysing research from overlapping disciplines. The next layer of transdisciplinary work will require teams of researchers from different disciplines to come together with stakeholders and interest groups in practical contexts to collaboratively explore complexities that influence and underlie how diverse groups think, feel, behave and plan around languages in their lives and what this means for social cohesion. For this purpose, we transformed the knowledge and insights we gained from our transdisciplinary literature review into an accessible set of questions guided by our framework of perspectives (Figure 5.1). These questions, compiled in Table 5.1, have been formulated to inspire dialogue and raise awareness of language-related possibilities and potential opportunities, as well as risks and challenges related to a conceptualisation of social cohesion that takes the language factor – in its complexity – into consideration. Any such discussions can be deepened and informed by consulting the research examples and themes (Chapter 4) that underpin our transdisciplinary language and social cohesion framework (Figure 5.1), and the EndNote library of article references made available online.

At this point, it is important to reiterate that the work we present in this book does not offer causal explanations; instead, it proposes a new conceptualisation that invites reflection, discussion and exploration of *possible* interconnections, influences and outcomes. It is designed to prompt interested parties to consider ideas, possibilities and warning signs that emerged from our literature review, when exploring other real-life practical contexts and research projects. We would like to emphasise here that the questions in Table 5.1 are based on evidence produced prior to the COVID-19 pandemic. Nevertheless, they continue to be valid as they are formulated to be applicable to diverse and changing contexts and situations. In addition, the list we compiled should not be understood as conclusive. Questions will need to be added and adapted, as we learn more about the perspectives related to social cohesion and languages. Such ongoing explorative and transdisciplinary engagement, supported by this book, could be of interest to a wide variety of actors and stakeholders, including people and teams with responsibilities within groups (e.g. sports and youth clubs), institutions (e.g. educational and religious institutions, companies, organisations) and authorities (e.g. ministries, NGOs, supranational bodies), as well as those who seek to research in these contexts.

To sum up, the thematic analysis and the ensuing framework of perspectives, together with the accessible tools of the questions and the EndNote Library, constitute our original contribution to knowledge and practice. In Table 5.1, the lines between the perspectives and dimensions are broken on purpose to indicate that only limited understanding can be gained from a single angle and that these perspectives should be embraced as intermeshed, as visualised in Figure 5.1.

Final words

Returning to our starting point, namely that we are writing this book at a particular time in history, much has changed since we started the project in 2018. We currently live in a world in which social contacts are shaped by COVID-19 restrictions. These have shifted the ways in which we maintain and build social relationships in the local, national, global, and particularly in the digital sphere. In many contexts, ideological divides continue to polarise societies, an economic crisis due to the COVID-19 pandemic is looming and meanwhile the climate crisis is building.

Given the current geopolitical developments, we feel that there is an ever greater need to examine social cohesion from all available angles and that language factors are an important part of any such equation. This has become clear through our analysis, as we have shown that languages and language varieties are arguably always present and relevant when questions of social cohesion arise in linguistically diverse contexts – as they are a precondition for communication and meaningful collaboration. Thus, through in-depth exploration of the role of languages, this book complements the guiding questions provided in the highly relevant UNDP (2020) report on social cohesion.

Given that linguistic diversity will inevitably continue to increase with globalisation and considering the huge, interconnected challenges the planet faces in the near future, with social divisions and increased voluntary and forced migration being one of them, transdisciplinary approaches such as the one we propose could pave the way to develop greater awareness of the conditions that facilitate or hinder meaningful contact and mediation between language groups. This may enable stakeholders to better support respectful and meaningful collaboration in situations where groups with multiple languages and diverse viewpoints do not simply coexist, but come together to negotiate their differences and identify shared goals in the interest of the common good.

Table 5.1 Interconnected language and social cohesion perspectives: Questions

Interconnected perspectives and dimensions to explore		Questions to explore social cohesion in particular language contact situations
Contextual	Language contexts	• What languages are visible and heard in society? Who uses these? • In what way do linguistic and other sociodemographic boundaries overlap, e.g. religion, social class? • Which groups have an interest in social cohesion and languages and why? • Is there a debate about languages or about language use? Which language groups have a voice in this?
	Conflicts and tensions between language groups	• Have there been conflicts in or between language groups? More recently and/or historically? • Have these conflicts been about language or about something else, e.g. empowerment of certain social groups? • Do certain groups feel their language is under threat?
	Opportunities for interaction between language groups	• What opportunities are there for positive contact and collaboration across language groups? • What type of societal opportunities exist to practice single or multiple languages?

(*continued*)

Table 5.1 Cont.

Interconnected perspectives and dimensions to explore		Questions to explore social cohesion in particular language contact situations
Distributive	Societal language resources	• What language resources do people have at what level? • In what way do language repertoires differ demographically?
	Distribution of language resources	• What educational opportunities exist for diverse social groups to develop their language repertoires? • Which groups can and do access these? Is there a choice?
	Resources available through languages	• What other resources can be accessed/ not accessed because of language competences or a lack thereof? • What emotional and practical resources can be obtained through languages by different groups? (In minority, majority, local, national, global language groups?)
Ideational	Language norms, values and beliefs	• How are *dominant, minority, foreign* and *other* languages valued, by whom and why? • Which languages and varieties are perceived as inferior or superior? In which context and by whom? • Which languages and varieties are perceived as normal and not normal? By whom? • What label is given to which language (*first, native, dominant, minority, migrant, majority, foreign* languages, *dialect, accent* and *lingua francas*)? And how are these evaluated by different groups? • What assumptions are associated with bi/multilingualism? Is there a difference if *foreign* and/or *community* languages are form part of such bi/multilingualism? • Is linguistic diversity seen as positive force or as a threat? By whom? • Are local *vernaculars* or *dialects* valued or considered as important for social belonging, especially in young people? • What (linguistic) groups are popularly seen as a problems related to social cohesion?

Table 5.1 Cont.

Interconnected perspectives and dimensions to explore		Questions to explore social cohesion in particular language contact situations
	Language expectations	• Which groups are expected to make a linguistic effort? For what purpose? • What languages are citizens/group members expected to learn, maintain or forget? For what purpose? • What languages and language varieties are deemed acceptable in different contexts (private, public, etc.)? • In what way do users of a shared language also share norms? Are there cultural differences? • Are language provisions viewed and sought after equally by different language groups? Which language learning preferences exist in different groups? Does this segregate learner groups? • Are bi-/multilingual group members given opportunities, or are they expected, to mediate between language groups? Are they supported in this? Are they happy to engage in mediation?
Emotional	Allegiances with language groups	• Are there social groups who identify with multiple language groups? • Are there social groups who identify with one language group only to the exclusion of others? Are these majority or minority groups? How is this allegiance communicated? • Are certain languages and varieties markers of allegiance with *minority, dominant, foreign, lingua franca* and *other* linguistic groups?
	Contested belonging to language groups	• What sense of belonging do linguistic groups desire and/or imagine? And why? • What sense of belonging do linguistic groups resist, contest and/or deny? And why? • In what ways is belonging to a certain language group invited, supported or rejected? By which groups and why? • Are there groups who desire to belong to one or multiple language groups, but struggle to gain access?

(continued)

Table 5.1 Cont.

Interconnected perspectives and dimensions to explore		Questions to explore social cohesion in particular language contact situations
Behavioural	Types of social networks between language groups	• What type of networks (weak, strong, vertical, horizontal) do people build based on their linguistic repertoire? • What weak ties exist/do not exist across linguistic and cultural communities? • What translingual weak ties are established? Through which languages? • Are strong networks established through a certain language? Are they supportive and/or exclusive in nature? • Are there groups who maintain ties with only one language group? Is this structurally determined or desired? • Are there groups who maintain ties to multiple language groups? Who are these groups? • How are languages and varieties used to build vertical networks between community and institutions/authority? • How are languages and varieties used to maintain inter-generational networks?
	Mediation between language groups	• What is the role of bi-/multilingual brokers and mediators between language groups? • Are there multilingual role models who model collaboration between language groups? • In what way is respect for languages and/ or language diversity manifest?
	Inclusion/ exclusion of language groups	• What networks do not exist because of a lack of languages? • How do people use languages to include or separate groups, e.g. through separate/ integrated language? • Are there other barriers to building networks within and between language groups?
Organisational	Language status planning for social cohesion	• In which ways are languages, monolingualism or multilingualism valued or not valued through policies/ frameworks/projects? • What norms and beliefs about language (and social) groups are perpetuated/ transformed by language decisions at policy/framework/project level?

Table 5.1 Cont.

Interconnected perspectives and dimensions to explore	Questions to explore social cohesion in particular language contact situations
	• Has language diversity been considered and discussed, or is a laissez-faire approach adopted? Why? • Are language decisions or compromises practical and affordable? Are they likely to be acceptable to different stakeholder and interest groups? • Might giving more/taking away language rights to one group polarise society? • How can any negative perceptions of language groups be addressed?
Language acquisition planning for social cohesion	• What language acquisition provisions are available? Which social groups are expected to access these? • What language maintenance provisions are available? Which social groups are expected to access these? • In what way do curricula support the development of language repertoires? • What language criteria enable access to educational institutions/streams? Do they (dis)advantage some social groups? • Are curricula supporting language learning, well-being and social cohesion as a political aim?
Language mediation planning	• What policies/frameworks/projects are in place to help groups communicate across language boundaries, locally, nationally and internationally? • What common goals or purposes are supported that encourages/discourages social groups to meaningfully communicate within and across linguistic boundaries?

Source: This framework and questions are the result of our transdisciplinary literature review (see Chapters 2 and 4).

Note

1 If readers cannot access the EndNote library, they can contact the lead author to obtain the list in a different format.

References

Acker-Hocevar, M., Cruz-Janzen, M., Wilson, C. L., Schoon, P., & Walker, D. (2006). The need to reestablish schools as dynamic positive human energy systems that are non-linear and self-organizing: The learning partnership tree. *International Journal of Learning, 12*(10), 255–267. https://doi.org/ 10.18848/1447-9494/CGP/v12i10/48216

Agha, A. (2007). *Language and social relations.* Cambridge University Press. https://doi.org/10.1017/CBO9780511618284

Albirini, A. (2013). Toward understanding the variability in the language proficiencies of Arabic heritage speakers. *International Journal of Bilingualism, 18*(6), 730–765. https://doi.org/10.1177/1367006912472404

Allport, G. (1954). *The nature of prejudice.* Addison-Wesley. https://doi.org/ 10.2307/3791349

Alonso, J. A., Durand, J., & Gutiérrez, R. (2014). Persistencia del español en los colectivos hispanos de los Estados Unidos. *Revista Internacional de Lingüística Iberoamericana, 12*(2), 39–58.

Alsagoff, L. (2010). English in Singapore: Culture, capital and identity in linguistic variation. *World Englishes, 29*(3), 336–348. https://doi.org/10.1111/ j.1467-971X.2010.01658.x

Amin, A. (2002). Ethnicity and the multicultural city: Living with diversity. *Environment and Planning A: Economy and Space.* https://doi.org/ 10.1068%2Fa3537

Amit, K., & Bar-Lev, S. (2015). Immigrants' sense of belonging to the host country: The role of life satisfaction, language proficiency, and religious motives. *Social Indicators Research, 124*(3), 947–961. https://doi.org/10.1007/ s11205-014-0823-3

Amos, Y. T. (2008). Stereotypes in disguise: The dual school lives of Japanese immigrant students. *International Journal of Multicultural Education, 10*(1), 959–980. https://doi.org/10.18251/ijme.v10i1.32

Anderson, B. (1983). *Imagined communities – reflections on the origins and spread of nationalism.* Verso.

Angermuller, J., & Glady, M. (2017). La sociologie du langage. Perspectives d'un champ émergent. *Langage et société, 160–161*(2), 163–178. https://doi. org/10.3917/ls.160.0163.

Anya, U. (2011). Connecting with communities of learners and speakers: Integrative ideals, experiences, and motivations of successful black second language learners. *Foreign Language Annals*, *44*(3), 441–466. https://doi.org/10.1111/j.1944-9720.2011.01142.x

Arriaza, G. (2004). Making changes that stay made: School reform and community involvement. *The High School Journal*, *87*(4), 10–24. https://doi.org/10.1353/hsj.2004.0007

Atindogbé, G., & Ebongue, A. (Eds.). (2019). *Linguistic and sociolinguistic perspectives of youth language practices in Africa: Codes and identity writings*. Langaa. https://doi.org/10.2307/j.ctvx07820

Atkinson, D. (2011). A sociocognitive approach to second language acquisition: How mind, body, and world work together in learning additional languages. In D. Atkinson (Ed.), *Alternative approaches to second language acquisition*, 143–166. Routledge.

Avineri, N., Graham, L. R., Johnson, E. J., Riner, R. C., & Rosa, J. (2019). *Language and social justice in practice*. Routledge. https://doi.org/10.4324/9781315115702

Baker, C. (2006). *Foundations of bilingual education and bilingualism* (4th ed.). Multilingual Matters.

Bankston, C. L., & Zhou, M. (1995). Effects of minority-language literacy on the academic achievement of Vietnamese youths in New Orleans. *Sociology of Education*, *68*(1), 1–17. https://doi.org/10.2307/2112760

Basford, L. (2010). From mainstream to East African Charter: Cultural and religious experiences of Somali youth in U.S. schools. *Journal of School Choice*, *4*(4), 485–509. https://doi.org/10.1080/15582159.2010.526859

Beech, J. (2009). Policy spaces, mobile discourses, and the definition of educated identities. *Comparative Education*, *45*(3), 347–364. https://doi.org/10.1080/03050060903184932

Beneke, M., & Cheatham, G. A. (2015). Speaking up for African American English: Equity and inclusion in early childhood settings. *Early Childhood Education Journal*, *43*(2), 127–134. https://doi.org/10.1007/s10643-014-0641-x

Berg, C., & Weis, C. (2007). *Réajustement de l'enseignment des langues: Plan d'action 2007–2009*. Éditions du CESIJE.

Berns, M., & Matsuda, K. (2006). Applied linguistics: Overview and history. In K. Brown (Ed.), *Encyclopedia of Language & Linguistics*, 2nd ed., pp. 394–405. Elsevier. https://doi.org/10.1016/B0-08-044854-2/00599-X

Bibri, S. E. (2021). The core academic and scientific disciplines underlying data-driven smart sustainable urbanism: An interdisciplinary and transdisciplinary framework. *Computational Urban Science*, *1*(1). https://doi.org/10.1007/s43762-021-00001-2

Bicchieri, C. (2005). The grammar of society: The nature and dynamics of social norms (pp. ix–xiv). Cambridge University Press. https://doi.org/10.1017/CBO9780511616037.001

Blackledge, A. (2001). The wrong sort of capital? Bangladeshi women and their children's schooling in Birmingham, U.K. *International Journal of*

Bilingualism, 5(3), 345–369. https://doi.org/10.1177%2F136700690100 50030501

Blackledge, A. (2004). Constructions of identity in political discourse in multilingual Britain. In A. Pavlenko, & A. Blackledge (Eds.), *Negotiation of identity in multilingual contexts*, 93–124. Multilingual Matters. https://doi.org/10.21832/9781853596483

Block, D. (2007). The rise of identity in SLA research, post Firth and Wagner (1997). *The Modern Language Journal, 91*, 863–876. https://doi.org/10.1111/j.1540-4781.2007.00674.x

Blommaert, J. (2006). Language Ideology. *Encyclopedia of Language & Linguistics, 6*, 510–522. https://doi.org/10.1016/B0-08-044854-2/03029-7

Blommaert, J. (2010). *The sociolinguistics of globalization.* Cambridge University Press. https://doi.org/10.1017/CBO9780511845307

Blommaert, J., & Verschueren, J. (1998). *Debating diversity. Analysing the discourse of tolerance.* Routledge. https://doi.org/10.4324/9780203029275

Bolívar, J. M., & Chrispeels, J. H. (2011). Enhancing parent leadership through building social and intellectual capital. *American Educational Research Journal, 48*(1), 4–38. https://doi.org/10.3102/0002831210366466

Booth, A., Papaioannou, D., & Sutton, A. (2012). *Systematic approaches to a successful literature review.* Sage.

Bourdieu, P. (1986). The forms of capital. In J. Richardson (Ed.), *Handbook of theory and research for the sociology of education.* Greenwood.

Bourdieu, P. (1991). *Language and symbolic power.* Polity Press.

Bourdieu, P., & Thompson, J. B. (1991). *Language and symbolic power.* Harvard University Press.

Bourhis, R. Y., Montaruli, E., El-Geledi, S., Harvey, S. P., & Barrette, G. (2010). Acculturation in multiple host community settings. *Journal of Social Issues, 66*(4), 780–802. https://doi.org/10.1111/j.1540-4560.2010.01675.x

Brady, J. (2015). Dialect, power and politics: Standard English and adolescent identities. *Literacy, 49*(3), 149–157. https://doi.org/10.1111/lit.12058

Branscombe, N. R., & Baron, R. A. (2017). *Social psychology* (14th ed). Pearson.

Brown, K. (2008). Regional identity and schools in Estonia: Creating a "we" feeling? *European Education, 40*(3), 8–26. https://doi.org/10.2753/EUE1056-4934400301

Brown, K. (2011). The influence of education on violent conflict and peace: Inequality, opportunity and the management of diversity. *Prospects, 41*(2), 191–204. https://doi.org/10.1007/s11125-011-9186-6

Brown, K. (2018). *Global issues are connected and that matters.* United Nations Foundation. https://unfoundation.org/blog/post/global-issues-connected-matters/

Brumfit, C. (1995). Teacher professionalism and research. In G. Cook, & B. Seidlhofer (Eds.), *Principle and practice in applied linguistics.* Oxford University Press.

Busch, B. (2012). The linguistic repertoire revisited. *Applied Linguistics, 33*(5), 503–523. https://doi.org/10.1093/applin/ams056

Butorac, D. (2014). 'Like the fish not in water': How language and race mediate the social and economic inclusion of women migrants to Australia. *Australian Review of Applied Linguistics, 37*(3), 234–248. https://doi.org/10.1075/aral.37.3.03but

Byram, M., Nichols, A., & Stevens, D. (2001). *Developing intercultural competence in practice.* Multilingual Matters. https://doi.org/10.21832/9781853595356

Caldas, S. J., & Cornigans, L. (2015). Race/Ethnicity and social capital among middle- and upper-middle-class elementary school families: A structural equation model. *School Community Journal, 25*(1), 137–156.

Canagarajah, S. (2013). *Translingual practice: Global Englishes and cosmopolitan relations.* Routledge.

Cantle, T. (2006). *Review of community cohesion in Oldham: Challenging local communities to change Oldham.* Oldham Council. www.oldham.gov.uk/cantle-review-final-report.pdf

Cantle, T. (2012). *Interculturalism: The new era of cohesion and diversity.* Palgrave Macmillan. https://doi.org/10.1111%2Fj.2041-9066.2012.00124.x

Carhill-Poza, A. (2017). "If you don't find a friend in here, it's gonna be hard for you": Structuring bilingual peer support for language learning in urban high schools. *Linguistics and Education, 37*, 63–72. https://doi.org/https://doi.org/10.1016/j.linged.2016.09.001

Carroll, T. F., & Bebbington, A. J. (2000). Peasant federations and rural development policies in the Andes. *Policy Sciences, 33*(3), 435–457. https://doi.org/10.1023/a:1004824803848

Carter, P. L. (2006). Straddling boundaries: Identity, culture, and school. *Sociology of Education, 79*(4), 304–328. https://doi.org/10.1177/003804070607900402

Cenoz, J., Gorter, D., & May, S. (Eds.). (2017). *Language awareness and multilingualism. Encyclopedia of language and education* (3rd ed.). Springer International Publishing. https://doi.org/10.1007/978-3-319-02240-6_1

Chan, E. (2002). Beyond pedagogy: Language and identity in post-colonial Hong Kong. *British Journal of Sociology of Education, 23*(2), 271–285. https://doi.org/10.1080/01425690220137756

Chan, J., To, H.P., & Chan, E. (2006). Reconsidering social cohesion: Developing a definition and analytical framework for empirical research. *Social Indicators Research, 75*, 273–302. https://doi.org/10.1007/sl 1205-005-2118-1

Chao, X., & Kuntz, A. (2013). Church-based ESL program as a figured world: Immigrant adult learners, language, identity, power. *Linguistics and Education, 24*, 466–478. https://doi.org/10.1016/j.linged.2013.06.001

Chávez, S. (2005). Community, ethnicity, and class in a changing rural California town. *Rural Sociology, 70*(3), 314–335. https://doi.org/10.1526/0036011054831224

Chen, S. C. (1997). Sociology of language. In N. H. Hornberger, & D. Corson (Eds.), *Encyclopedia of language and education*, Vol. 8, 1–13. Springer. https://doi.org/10.1007/978-94-011-4535-0_1

Chen, X., Stanton, B., Kaljee, L. M., Fang, X., Xiong, Q., Lin, D., Zhang, L., & Li, X. (2011). Social stigma, social capital reconstruction, and rural migrants in urban China: A population health perspective. *Human Organization*, *70*(1), 22–32. https://doi.org/10.17730/humo.70.1.k76047734m703500

Chen, Y. (2010). Boarding school for Uyghur students: Speaking Uyghur as a bonding social capital. *Diaspora, Indigenous, and Minority Education*, *4*(1), 4–16. https://doi.org/10.1080/15595690903442231

Cheong, P. H., Edwards, R., Goulbourne, H., & Solomos, J. (2007). Immigration, social cohesion and social capital: A critical review. *Critical Social Policy*, *27*(1), 24–49. https://doi.org/10.1177/0261018307072206

Chong, A., Guillen, J., & Rios, V. (2010). Language nuances, trust and economic growth. *Public Choice*, *143*(1), 191–208. https://doi.org/10.1007/s11127-009-9497-9

Clyne, M. (2008). A linguist's vision for multicultural Australia. *Eureka Street*, *18*(23). www.eurekastreet.com.au/article/a-linguist-s-vision-for-multicultural-australia

Cok, L., & Novak-Lukanovic, S. (2004, November 18–20). *Languages as social cohesion and human capital* [Conference presentation]. 5th International Conference of the Faculty of Management, University of Primorska, Congress Centre Bernardin, Portorož, Slovenia. www.fm-kp.si/zalozba/ISBN/961-6486-71-3/079-089.pdf

Coleman, H. (Ed). (2011). *Dreams and realities: Developing countries and the English language* (Paper 2). British Council.

Coleman, J. S. (1988). Social capital in the creation of human capital. *American Journal of Sociology*, *94*, 95–120. https://doi.org/10.1086/228943

Conteh, J., & Meier, G. (2014). *The multilingual turn in languages and education: Opportunities and challenges*. Multilingual Matters.

Cook, G. (2003). *Applied linguistics*. Oxford University Press.

Copp Mökkönen, A. (2013). Newcomers navigating language choice and seeking voice: Peer talk in a multilingual primary school classroom in Finland. *Anthropology and Education*, *44*(2), 124–141. https://doi.org/10.1111/aeq.12011

Corbett, J. (2020). Revisiting mediation: Implications for intercultural language education. *Language and Intercultural Communication*, *21*(1), 8–23 https://doi-org.uoelibrary.idm.oclc.org/10.1080/14708477.2020.1833897

Coste, D., Moore, D., & Zarate, G. (2009). *Plurilingual and pluricultural competence*. Council of Europe, Language Policy Division.

Council of Europe. (2001). *The Common European Framework of Reference for Languages (CEFR)*. Cambridge University Press.

Council of Europe. (2014). *Languages for democracy and social cohesion: Diversity, equity and quality*. Language Policy Unit. https://rm.coe.int/languages-for-democracy-and-social-cohesion-diversity-equity-and-quali/168069e7bd

Council of Europe. (2018). *Common European Framework of Reference for Languages: Learning, teaching, assessment (Companion volume with new descriptors*). Council of Europe. https://rm.coe.int/cefr-companion-volume-with-new-descriptors-2018/1680787989

Coyle, D., Holmes, B., & King, L. (2009). *Towards an integrated curriculum – CLIL national statement and guidelines*. The Languages Company.

Coyle, D., Hood, P., & Marsh, D. (2010). *CLIL*. Cambridge University Press. https://doi.org/10.1080/09500782.2010.539045

Creese, A., & Blackledge, A. (Eds.). (2014). Heteroglossia as practice and peda-gogy. In A. Blackledge, & A. Creese (Eds.), *Heteroglossia as practice and pedagogy*. Springer. https://doi.org/10.1007/978-94-007-7856-6_1

Crowley, H., & Hickman, M. (2008). Migration, postindustrialism and the globalized nation state: Social capital and social cohesion re-examined. *Ethnic and Racial Studies*, *31*(7), 1222–1244. https://doi.org/10.1080/01419870701725904

Cruickshank, K. (2014). Exploring the –lingual between bi and mono: Young people and their languages in an Australian context. In S. May (Ed.), *The multilingual turn: Implications for SLA, TESOL and bilingual education*. Routledge.

Cruickshank, K., Black, S., Chen, H., Tsung, L., & Wright, J. (2020). *Language education in the school curriculum: Issues of access and equity*. Bloomsbury Academic.

Cummins, J. (2019). Should schools undermine or sustain multilingualism? An analysis of theory, research, and pedagogical practice. *Darnioji daugiakal-bystė / Sustainable Multilingualism*, *15*, 1–26. doi.org/10.2478/sm-2019-0011

Cummins, J., Bismilla, V., Chow, V., Cohen, S., Giampapa, F., Leoni, L., & Sandhu, P. (2006). *ELL students speak for themselves: Identity texts and lit-eracy engagement in multilingual classrooms*. University of Toronto. https://research.steinhardt.nyu.edu/scmsAdmin/media/users/ccm246/Haynes_2010/ELLidentityTexts.pdf

Cunningham, U., & King, J. (2018). Language, ethnicity, and belonging for the children of migrants in New Zealand. *International Journal of Bilingualism*, *8*(2), 1–11. https://doi.org/10.1177%2F2158244018782571

Darquennes, J. (2015). Language conflict research: a state of the art. *International Journal of Sociology of Language*, *235*, 7–32. https://doi.org/10.1515/ijsl-2015-0012

Davis, C. P. (2015). Speaking conflict: Ideological barriers to bilingual policy implementation in civil war Sri Lanka. *Anthropology & Education Quarterly*, *46*(2), 95–112. https://doi.org/10.1111/aeq.12093

de Keere, K., & Elchardus, M. (2011). Narrating linguistic conflict: A story-telling analysis of the language conflict in Belgium. *Journal of Multilingual and Multicultural Development*, *32*(3), 221–234. https://doi.org /10.1080/01434632.2011.563857

De Saussure, F. (1966). *Course in general linguistics*. McGraw-Hill.

De Swaan, A. (2001). *Words of the world: The global language system*. Polity Press.

Deffa, O.-J. (2016). The impact of homogeneity on intra-group cohesion: A macro-level comparison of minority communities in a Western diaspora.

Journal of Multilingual and Multicultural Development, *37*(4), 343–356. https://doi.org/10.1080/01434632.2015.1072203

Dei, S. G. J. (2005). Social difference and the politics of schooling in Africa: A Ghanaian case study. *Compare: A Journal of Comparative and International Education*, *35*(3), 227–245. https://doi.org/10.1080/03057920500212522

Deneire, M. (2008). English in the French workplace: Realism and anxieties. *World Englishes*, *27*(2), 181–195. https://doi.org/10.1111/j.1467-971X.2008.00551.x

Dewaele, J. M., & van Oudenhoven, P. (2009). The effect of multilingualism/multiculturalism on personality: No gain without pain for third culture kids". *International Journal of Multilingualism*, *6*(4), 443–459. https://doi.org/10.1080/14790710903039906

Dijkers, M. (2015). What is a scoping review? *Knowledge Translation Update 4*(1). https://ktdrr.org/products/update/v4n1/dijkers_ktupdate_v4n1_12-15.pdf

Doerr, N. (2004). Desired division, disavowed division: An analysis of the labeling of the bilingual unit as separatist in an Aotearoa/New Zealand school. *Anthropology & Education Quarterly*, *35*(2), 233–253. https://doi.org/10.1525/aeq.2004.35.2.233

Donnelly, M., Barratta, A., & Gamsu, S. (2019). A sociolinguistic perspective on accent and social mobility in the UK teaching profession. *Sociological Research Online*, *24*(4), 496–513. https://doi.org/10.1177/1360780418816335

Dörnyei, Z., & Ushioda, E. (Eds.). (2009). *Motivation, language identity and the L2 self* (pp. 9–41). Multilingual Matters.

Duchêne, A., & Heller, M. (Eds.). (2007). *Discourses of endangerment: Ideology and interest in the defence of languages*. Continuum.

Duff, P., & Talmy, S. (2011). Language socialization approaches to second language acquisition: Social, cultural, and linguistic development in additional languages. In D. Atkinson (Ed.), *Alternative approaches to second language acquisition*, 95–116. Routledge. https://doi.org/10.4324/9780203830932

Edwards, C. W. (2016). Language-in-education policies, immigration and social cohesion in Catalonia: The case of Vic. *International Journal of Bilingual Education and Bilingualism*, *19*(5), 530–545. https://doi.org/10.1080/13670050.2015.1023253

Ender, A., & Straßl, K. (2009). The acquisition and use of German in a dialect-speaking environment: facets of inclusion and exclusion of immigrant children in Switzerland. *International Journal of Applied Linguistics*, *19*(2), 173–187. https://doi.org/10.1111/j.1473-4192.2009.00218.x

Estrada-Martínez, L. M., Padilla, M. B., Caldwell, C. H., & Schulz, A. J. (2011). Examining the influence of family environments on youth violence: A comparison of Mexican, Puerto Rican, Cuban, Non-Latino black, and Non-Latino white Adolescents. *Journal of Youth and Adolescence*, *40*(8), 1039–1051. https://doi.org/10.1007/s10964-010-9624-4

Extra, G., & Gorter, D. (2001). *The other languages of Europe*. Multilingual Matters.

Field, J. (2003). *Social capital: Key ideas*. Routledge.

Fishman, J., & García, O. (2010). *Handbook of language and ethnic identity*. Oxford, University Press.

Flores, N. (2015). A tale of two visions: Hegemonic whiteness and bilingual education. *Educational Policy, 30*(1), 13–38. https://doi.org/10.1177/0895904815616482

Fotovatian, S. (2015). Language, institutional identity and integration: Lived experiences of ESL teachers in Australia. *Globalisation, Societies and Education, 13*(2), 230–245. https://doi.org/10.1080/14767724.2014.934072

Fouka, V. (2016). Backlash: The unintended effects of language prohibition in US Schools after World War I. *Stanford Center for International Development Working Paper, 591*. Stanford University.

Friedkin, N. E. (2004). Social cohesion. *Annual Review of Sociology, 30*, 409–425. https://doi.org/10.1146/annurev.soc.30.012703.110625

Friedman, D. (2010). Becoming national: Classroom language socialization and political identities in the age of globalization. *Annual Review of Applied Linguistics, 30*, 193–210. https://doi.org/10.1017/S0267190510000061

Gagnon, C. (2006). Language plurality as power struggle: Translating politics in Canada. *Target, 18*(1), 69–90. https://doi.org/10.1075/target.18.1.05gag

Gajo, L. (2014). From normalization to didactization of multilingualism: European and francophone research at the crossroads between linguistics and didactics. In J. Conteh, & G. Meier (Eds.), *The multilingual turn in languages education: Opportunities and challenges*, 113–131. Multilingual Matters.

Ganek, H., Nixon, S., Smyth, R., & Eriks-Brophy, A. (2019). A cross-cultural mixed methods investigation of language socialization practices. *Journal of Deaf Studies and Deaf Education, 24*(2), 128–141. https://doi.org/10.1093/deafed/eny037

García, O., & Sylvan, C. E. (2011). Pedagogies and practices in multilingual classrooms: Singularities in pluralities. *The Modern Language Journal, 95*(iii), 385–400. https://doi.org/10.1111/j.1540-4781.2011.01208.x

García, O., & Wei, L. (2014). *Translanguaging: Language, bilingualism and education*. Palgrave Macmillan.

Garrett, P. B., & Baquedano-López, P. (2002). Language socialization: Reproduction and continuity, transformation and change. *Annual Review of Anthropology, 31*, 339–361. https://doi.org/10.1146/annurev.anthro.31.040402.085352

Gast, M. J., Okamoto, D. G., & Feldman, V. (2017). "We only speak English here": English dominance in language diverse, immigrant after-school programs. *Journal of Adolescent Research, 32*(1), 94–121. https://doi.org/10.1177/0743558416674562

Gerhards, J. (2014). Transnational linguistic capital: Explaining English proficiency in 27 European countries. *International Sociology, 29*(1), 56–74. https://doi.org/10.1177/0268580913519461

Giardello, M. (2014). The generative theory of social cohesion and civic integration. *European Scientific Journal, 2*, 80–89.

Giuliano, E. (2000). Who determines the self in the politics of self-determination? Identity and preference formation in Tatarstan's nationalist mobilization. *Comparative Politics, 32*(3), 295–316. https://doi.org/10.2307/422368

Goglia, F., & Fincati, V. (2017). Immigrant languages and the Veneto dialect in the linguistic repertoires of secondary school pupils of immigrant origin in the Veneto region. *Studi Italiani di Linguistica Teorica ed Applicata, XLV,* 497–517.

Gogolin, I. (1994). *Der monolinguale Habitus der multilingualen Schule.* Waxman.

Gomolla, M., & Radtke, F. O. (2007). *Institutionelle Diskriminierung: Die Herstellung ethnischer Differenz in der Schule.* VS Verlag für Sozialwissenschaften.

González-Davies, M. (2020). Developing mediation competence through translation. In S. Laviosa, & M. González-Davies (Eds.), *The Routledge handbook of translation and education,* 434–450. Routledge. https://doi.org/10.4324/9780367854850

Goundar, P. R. (2017). The characteristics of language policy and planning research: An overview. In X. Jiang (Ed.), *Sociolinguistics: interdisciplinary perspectives.* Intechopen. https://doi.org/10.5772/intechopen.68152

Granovetter, M. (1973). The Strength of Weak Ties. *American Journal of Sociology, 78,* 1360–1380. https://doi.org/10.1086/225469

Granovetter, M. (1983). The strength of weak ties: a network theory revisited. *Sociological Theory, 1,* 201–233. https://doi.org/10 2307202051.

Green, A., Preston, J., & Janmaat, J.G. (2006). *Education, equality and social cohesion.* Palgrave Macmillan.

Grix, J. (2001). Towards a theoretical approach to the study of cross-border cooperation. *Perspectives, 17,* 5–13.

Grosjean, F. (1982). *Life with two languages. An introduction to bilingualism.* Harvard University Press.

Guilherme, M. (2002). *Critical citizens for an intercultural world: Foreign language education as cultural politics.* Multilingual Matters.

Gundara, J. S. (2000). Issues of discrimination in European education systems. *Comparative Education, 36*(2), 223–234. https://doi.org/10.1080/713656608

Guo, Y. (2011). Beyond deficit paradigms: Exploring informal learning of immigrant parents. *The Canadian Journal for the Study of Adult Education, 24*(1), 41–59.

Gutman, A. (Ed.) (1994). *Multiculturalism: Examining the politics of recognition.* Princeton University Press.

Haarmann, H. (1990). Elements of a theory of language conflict. In Peter H. Nelde (Ed.), *Language attitudes and language conflict* (Plurilingua IX), 1–15. Dümmler.

Halliday, M. A. K. (1985). *An introduction to functional grammar.* Edward Arnold.

Hamid, M. O., & Jahan, I. (2015). Language, identity, and social divides: Medium of instruction debates in Bangladeshi print media. *Comparative Education Review, 59*(1), 75–101. https://doi.org/10.1086/679192

Han, H. (2011). Social inclusion through multilingual ideologies, policies and practices: A case study of a minority church. *International Journal of Bilingual Education and Bilingualism, 14*(4), 383–398. https://doi.org/10.1080/13670050.2011.573063

Harvey, N., & Myint, H. H. (2014). Our language is like food: Can children feed on home languages to thrive, belong and achieve in early childhood education and care? *Australasian Journal of Early Childhood, 39*(2), 42–50. https://doi.org/10.1177/183693911403900207

Heikkinen, S. J. (2011). Exclusion of older immigrants from the former Soviet Union to Finland: The meaning of intergenerational relationships. *Journal Cross-Cultural Gerontology, 26*(4), 379–395. https://doi.org/10.1007/s10823-011-9153-y

Hejwowski, H. (2018). Applied linguistics and translation studies. *Crossroads: A Journal of English Studies, 21*(2), 4–10. https://doi.org/10.15290/cr.2018.21.2.01

Hermans, P. (2006). Counternarratives of Moroccan parents in Belgium and the Netherlands: Answering back to discrimination in education and society. *Ethnography and Education, 1*(1), 87–101. https://doi.org/10.1080/17457820500512846

Higgins, C., & Stoker, K. (2011). Language learning as a site for belonging: A narrative analysis of Korean adoptee-returnees. *International Journal of Bilingual Education and Bilingualism, 14*(4), 399–412. https://doi.org/10.1080/13670050.2011.573064

Hintermann, C., Markom, C., Weinhäupl, H., & Üllen, S. (2014). Debating migration in textbooks and classrooms in Austria. *Journal of Educational Media, Memory, and Society, 6*(1), 79–106. https://doi.org/10.3167/jemms.2014.060105

Hirsch Hadorn, G., Hoffmann-Riem, H., Biber-Klemm, S., Grossenbacher-Mansuy, W., Joye, D., Pohl, C., Wiesmann, U., & Zemp, E. (2008). (Eds.), *Handbook of Transdisciplinary Research (pp. 399-410)*. Springer Netherlands.

Ho, J. W. Y. (2008). Code Choice in Hong Kong: From bilingualism to trilingualism. *Australian Review of Applied Linguistics 31*(2). 18.1-18.17.

Hogan-Brun, G., & O'Rourke, B. (Eds.). (2019). *The Palgrave handbook of minority languages and communities*. Springer.

Holland, J. (2009). Young people and social capital: Uses and abuses? *Young, 17*(4), 330–350. https://doi.org/10.1177%2F110330880901700401

Hu, G. (2008). The misleading academic discourse on Chinese-English bilingual education in China. *Review of Educational Research, 78*(1), 190–226. https://doi.org/10.3102/0034654307313406

Ibarra, W., & Calderón, E. (2016). Educação intercultural bilíngue no Chile. *Revista Brasileira de História da Educação, 16*(3), 288–322. https://doi.org/10.4025/rbhe.v16i3.785

Irvine, J. T. (1989). When talk isn't cheap: Language and political economy. *American Ethnologist, 16*, 248–267.

Jacobone, V., & Moro, G. (2015). Evaluating the impact of the Erasmus Programme: Skills and European identity. *Assessment & Evaluation in Higher Education, 40*(2), 309–328. https://doi.org/10.1080/02602938.2014.909005

Jenson, J. (2019). Intersections of pluralism and social cohesion: Two concepts for the practice of pluralism. *Intersections: Practicing Pluralism.* Global Centre for Pluralism.

Joy, R., & Murphy, E. (2012). The inclusion of children with special educational needs in an intensive French as a second-language program: From theory to practice. *Canadian Journal of Education, 35*(1), 102–119.

Kalocsányiová, E. (2018). At the borders of languages: the role of ideologies in the integration of forced migrants in multilingual Luxembourg. *Journal of Ethnic and Migration Studies, 46*(3), 1–18. https://doi.org/10.1080/1369183X.2018.1510307

Kameyama, S., & Meyer, B. (Eds.). (2007). *Mehrsprachigkeit am Arbeitsplatz.* Peter Lang.

Kearns, A., & Forrest, R. (2000). Social cohesion and multilevel urban governance. *Urban Studies, 37*(5–6), 995–1017. https://doi.org/10.1080/00420980050011208

Kelleher, A., & Ryan, K. (2012). Successful local peacebuilding in Macedonia: Sustained dialogue in practice. *Peace Research, 44*(1), 63–94.

Kelly, C. (2011). A critical pedagogy of cafeterias and communities: The power of multiple voices in diverse settings. *Middle Grades Research Journal, 62*(2), 97–111.

Kelly, M. (2009). A third space for Europe: Intercultural communication in European language policy. *European Journal of Language Policy, 1*(1), 1.

Kheimets, N. G., & Epstein, A. D. (2001). English as a central component of success in the professional and social integration of scientists from the former Soviet Union in Israel. *Language in Society, 30*(2), 187–215. https://doi.org/10.1017/S0047404501002020

Kioko, A. N., Ndung'u, R. W., & Mutiga, J. (2014). Mother tongue and education in Africa: Publicising the reality. *Multilingual Education, 4*(18). www.multilingual-education.com/content/4/1/1

Kirkpatrick, A. (2017). Language education policy among the Association of South East Asian Nations (ASEAN). *European Journal of Language Policy, 9*(1), 7–25.

Kitching, K. (2010). An excavation of the racialised politics of viability underpinning education policy in Ireland. *Irish Educational Studies, 29*(3), 213–229. https://doi.org/10.1080/03323315.2010.498278

Kostoulas-Makrakis, N., Karantzola, E., & Athanassiadis, E. (2006). Attitudes toward bilingualism: The case of two Greek islands. *Mediterranean Journal of Educational Studies, 11*(2), 17–34.

Kramsch, C. (2009). Third culture and language education. In V. Cook, L. Wei (Eds.), *Contemporary applied linguistics*, Vol. 1, 233–254. Continuum.

Kress, G., & Hodge, R. (1979). *Language as ideology.* Routledge and Kegan Paul.

Kubota, R. (2011). Learning a foreign language as leisure and consumption: Enjoyment, desire, and the business of "Eikaiwa". *International Journal* of *Bilingual Education and Bilingualism*, *14*(4), 473–488. https://doi.org/ 10.1080/13670050.2011.573069

Kumaravadivelu, B. (2005). *Understanding language teaching: From method to postmethod*. Lawrence Erlbaum Associates.

Kymlicka, W. (2011). Multicultural citizenship within multination states. *Ethnicities*, *11*(3), 281–302. https://doi.org/10.1177/1468796811407813

Labov, W. (1972). *Sociolinguistic patterns*. University of Pennsylvania Press.

La Placa, V., & Corlyon, J. (2014). Barriers to inclusion and successful engagement of parents in mainstream services: Evidence and research. *Journal of Children's Services*, *9*(3). https://doi.org/10.1108/JCS-05-2014-0027

Lamarre, P., Paquette, J., Kahn, E., & Ambrosi, S. (2002). Multilingual Montreal: Listening in on the language practices of young Montrealers. *Canadian Ethnic Studies Journal*, *34*(3), 47–75.

Lan, P.-C. (2011). White privilege, language capital and cultural ghettoisation: Western high-skilled migrants in Taiwan. *Journal of Ethnic and Migration Studies*, *37*(10), 1669–1693. https://doi.org/10.1080/ 1369183X.2011.613337

Langenkamp, A. G. (2005). Latino children's integration into American society: The dynamics of bilingual education. *Sociological Focus*, *38*(2), 115–131. https://doi.org/10.1080/00380237.2005.10571260

Lantolf, J. P. (2011). The sociocultural approach to second language acquisition: Sociocultural theory, second language acquisition, and artificial L2 development. In D. Atkinson (Ed.), *Alternative approaches to second language acquisition*, 24–47. Routledge.

Lavariega Monforti, J., & Sanchez, G. R. (2010). The politics of perception: An investigation of the presence and sources of perceptions of internal discrimination among Latinos. *Social Science Quarterly*, *91*(1), 245–265. https://doi. org/10.1111/j.1540-6237.2010.00691.x

Lee, J. D., Vera Sanchez, C. G., & Baba, Y. (2013). Sunday friends: The working alternative to charity. *Journal of Applied Social Science*, *7*(2), 148–187. https://doi.org/10.1177/1936724412475138

Lengyel. D. (2017). Stichwort: Mehrsprachigkeitsforschung. *Zeitschrift für Erziehungswissenschaft*, *20*(2), 153–174. https://doi.org/10.1007/ s11618-017-0734-6

Lesar, I., Čuk, I., & Peček, M. (2006). How to improve the inclusive orientation of Slovenian primary school—the case of Romani and migrant children from former Yugoslavia. *European Journal of Teacher Education*, *29*(3), 387–399. https://doi.org/10.1080/02619760600795262

Levinson, M. P. (2007). Literacy in English Gypsy communities: Cultural capital manifested as negative assets. *American Educational Research Journal*, *44*(1), 5–39. https://doi.org/10.3102/0002831206298174

Licona, M. (2013). Mexican and Mexican-American children's funds of knowledge as interventions into deficit thinking: Opportunities for praxis in science education. *Cultural Studies of Science Education*, *8*(4), 859–872. https://doi.org/10.1007/s11422-013-9515-6

Liddicoat, A. (2014). Pragmatics and intercultural mediation in intercultural language learning. *Intercultural Pragmatics*, *11*(2), 259–277. http://dx.doi.org/10.1515/ip-2014-0011

Lien, P. T., Conway, M., & Wong, J. (2003). The contours and sources of ethnic identity choices among Asian Americans. *Social Science Quarterly*, *84*(2), 461–481. https://doi.org/10.1111/1540-6237.8402015

Lin, N. (2001). *Social capital*. Cambridge University Press. https://doi.org/10.1017/CBO9780511815447

Lockwood, D. (1999). Civic integration and social cohesion. In I. Gough, & G. Olofsson (Eds.), *Capitalism and social cohesion: Essays on exclusion and integration*, 63–84. Palgrave Macmillan. https://doi.org/10.1057/9780230379138_4

Lopez, C. O., & Donovan, L. (2009). Involving Latino parents with mathematics through family math nights: A review of the literature. *Journal of Latinos and Education*, *8*(3), 219–230. https://doi.org/10.1080/15348430902888666

Luke, A. (2003). Literacy and the other: A sociological approach to literacy research and policy in multilingual societies. *Reading Research Quarterly*, *38*(1), 132–141.

Luna, N., & Revilla, A. T. (2013). Understanding Latina/o school pushout: Experiences of students who left school before graduating. *Journal of Latinos and Education*, *12*(1), 22–37. https://doi.org/10.1080/15348431.2012.734247

Lynch, A., Klee, C. A., & Tedick, D. J. (2001). Social factors and language proficiency in postsecondary Spanish immersion: Issues and implications. *Hispania, 84*(3), 510–524. https://doi.org/10.2307/3657811

Maalouf, A. (2008). *A rewarding challenge: How language diversity could strengthen Europe*. Directorate-General for Education, Youth, Sport and Culture (European Commission). https://op.europa.eu/en/publication-detail/-/publication/7f987cdd-dba2-42e7-8cdf-3f4f14efe783

Machado-Casas, M. (2009). The politics of organic phylogeny: The art of parenting and surviving as transnational multilingual Latino indigenous immigrants in the U.S. *High School Journal, 92*(4), 82–99. https://doi.org/10.1353/hsj.0.0034

May, S., & Hornberger, N. (2008). Language policy and political issues in education. In T. McCarty, & S.May (Eds.), *Encyclopedia of language and education*, Vol. 1. Springer Netherlands.

May, S. (Ed.). (2014). *The multilingual turn: Implications for SLA, TESOL and bilingual education*. Routledge.

McAllister, P. A. (1997). Cultural diversity and public policy in Australia and South Africa – The implications of 'multiculturalism'. *African Sociological Review / Revue Africaine de Sociologie, 1*(2), 60–78.

McIntosh, J. (2005). Language essentialism and social hierarchies among Giriama and Swahili. *Journal of Pragmatics, 37*, 1919–1944. https://doi.org/10.1016/j.pragma.2005.01.010

Meier, G. (2012a). Enseignement bilingue et l'amélioration des performances scolaires: Les conclusions de l'expérience Wix Primary School / École de Wix à Londres. *Synergies Europe, 7*, 53–75.

Meier, G. (2012b). Zweiwegintegration durch zweisprachige Bildung? Ergebnisse aus der Staatlichen Europa-Schule Berlin. *International Review of Education*, *58*(3), 335–352. https://doi.org/10.1007/s11159-012-9290-8

Meier, G. (2014). "Cette entraide et ce tutorat naturel qui s'organise entre eux": A research framework for two-way bilingual immersion programmes. In N. Morys, C. Kirsch, I. de Saint-Georges, & G. Gretsch (Eds.), *Lernen und lehren in multilingualen Kontexten: Zum Umgang mit sprachlich-kultureller Diversität im Klassenraum*. Peter Lang.

Meier, G. (2017). The multilingual turn as a critical movement in education: assumptions, challenges and a need for reflection. *Applied Linguistics Review*, *8*(1), 131–161. https://doi.org/10.1515/applirev-2016-2010

Meier, G. (2018). Multilingual socialisation in education: Introducing the M-SOC framework. *Language Education and Multilingualism – The Langscape Journal*, *1*(1), 103–125. https://doi.org/10.18452/19034

Meier, G., & Daniels, H. (2013). "Just not being able to make friends": Social interaction during the year abroad in modern language degrees. *Research Papers in Education*, *28*(2), 212–238. https://doi.org/10.1080/02671522.2011.629734

Meier, G., Smala, S., & Lawson, H. (2021). "Languages and Social Cohesion: A transdisciplinary literature review (Dataset)", Mendeley Data, Vol. 3, doi: 10.17632/ydtms99mjm.3. [download EndNote Library from: https://data.mendeley.com/datasets/ydtms99mjm/3]

Modood, T. (2007). Multiculturalism: A very short introduction. Oxford University Press.

Moher, D., Liberati, A., Tetzlaff, J., Altman, D.G., & The PRISMA Group. (2009). Preferred Reporting items for systematic reviews and meta-analyses: The PRISMA statement. *PLoS Medicine*, *6*(7). https://doi.org/10.1371/journal.pmed1000097

Molinsky, A. (2005). Language fluency and the evaluation of cultural faux pas: Russians interviewing for jobs in the United States. *Social Psychology Quarterly*, *68*(2), 103–120. https://doi.org/10.1177/019027250506800201

Montuori, A. (2013). Complexity and transdisciplinarity: Reflections on theory and practice. *World Futures*, *69*(4–6), 200–230. https://doi.org/10.1080/02604027.2013.803349

Moore, L. C. (2005). Language socialization. In A. Sujoldzic (Section Ed.), *Linguistic Anthropology, Encyclopedia of Life Support Systems (EOLSS)*. UNESCO.

Morales, A., & Hanson, W. E. (2005). Language brokering: An integrative review of the literature. *Hispanic Journal of Behavioral Sciences*, *27*(4), 471–503. https://doi.org/10.1177/0739986305281333

Musa, N. C., Lie, K. Y., & Azman, H. (2012). Exploring English language learning and teaching in Malaysia. *Journal of Language Studies*, 12, 35–52.

Nekvapil, J., & Sherman, T. (2015). An introduction: Language management theory in language policy and planning. *International Journal of Sociology of language*, *232*, 1–13.

Nelde, P. H. (1997). Language conflict. In F. Coulmas (Ed.), *The handbook of sociolinguistics*, 285–300. Blackwell.

Ng, P. C. L. (2012). English in the Singapore's Chinese community: Controversies, concerns and problems. *Journal of English as an International Language*, 7(1), 22–39.

NicCraith, M. (2000). Contested identities and the quest for legitimacy. *Journal of Multilingual and Multicultural Development*, 21(5), 399–413, https://doi.org/10.1080/01434630008666413

Norton, B. (2014). Identity, literacy, and the multilingual classroom. In S. May (Ed.), *The multilingual turn: Implications for SLA, TESOL, and bilingual education*, 103–122. Routledge.

Norton, B., & McKinney, C. (2011). An identity approach to second language acquisition. In D. Atkinson (Ed.), *Alternative approaches to second language acquisition*, 73–94. Routledge.

Norton, B., & Toohey, K. (2011). Identity, language learning, and social change. *Language Teaching*, 44, 412–446. https://doi.org/10.1017/S0261444811000309

Nyati-Saleshando, L. (2011). An advocacy project for multicultural education: The case of the Shiyeyi language in Botswana. *International Review of Education*, 57(5), 567–582. https://doi.org/10.1007/s11159-011-9254-4

Obasi, C. (2008). Seeing the deaf in "deafness". *Journal of Deaf Studies and Deaf Education*, 13(4), 455–465. https://doi.org/http://dx.doi.org/10.1093/deafed/enn008

Onwuegbuzie, A., & Frels, R. (2016). *Seven steps to a comprehensive literature review: A multimodal and cultural approach*. Sage.

Ortega, L. (2014). Ways forward for a bi/multilingual turn in SLA. In S. May (Ed.), *The multilingual turn: Implications for SLA, TESOL and bilingual education*, 32–53. Routledge.

Osler, A., & Lybaek, L. (2014). Educating 'the new Norwegian we': an examination of national and cosmopolitan education policy discourses in the context of extremism and islamophobia. *Oxford Review of Education*, 40(5), 543–566. https://doi.org/10.1080/03054985.2014.946896

Otsuji, E., & Pennycook, A. (2011). Social inclusion and metrolingual practices. *International Journal of Bilingual Education and Bilingualism*, 14(4), 413–426. https://doi.org/10.1080/13670050.2011.573065

Ovando, C. J. (2003). Bilingual education in the United States: Historical development and current issues. *Bilingual Research Journal*, 27(1), 1–24. https://doi.org/10.1080/15235882.2003.10162589

Patrick, D., & Tomiak, J.-A. (2008). Language, culture and community among urban Inuit in Ottawa. *Études/Inuit/Studies*, 32(1), 55–72. https://doi.org/10.7202/029819ar

Pavlenko, A., & Norton, B. (2007). Imagined communities, identity, and English learning. In J. Cummins & C. Davison (Eds.), *Springer international handbook of English language teaching*, 669–680. Springer.

Paxton, P. (2002). Social capital and democracy: An interdependent relationship. *American Sociological Review*, 67, 254–277. https://doi.org/10.2307/3088895

Pennycook, A.D. (2001). *Critical applied linguistics: A critical introduction.* Routledge. https://doi.org/10.4324/9781410600790

Petrovic, J. E. (1997). Balkanization, bilingualism, and comparisons of language situations at home and abroad. *Bilingual Research Journal, 21*(2–3), 233–254. https://doi.org/10.1080/15235882.1997.10668662

Phipps, A. M., & Fassetta, G. (2015). A critical analysis of language policy in Scotland. *European Journal of Language Policy, 7*(1), 5–27. https://doi.org/10.3828/ejlp.2015.2

Prins, E. (2007). Interdistrict transfers, Latino/White school segregation, and institutional racism in a small California town. *Journal of Latinos and Education, 6*(4), 285–308. https://doi.org/10.1080/15348430701473389

Pujolar, J. (2010). Immigration and language education in Catalonia: Between national and social agendas. *Linguistics and Education: An International Research Journal, 21*(3), 229–243. https://doi.org/10.1016/j.linged.2009.10.004

Putnam, R. (1996). Who killed civic America? *Prospect, 6*, 1–13.

Putnam, R. (2000). *Bowling Alone: The collapse and revival of American community.* Simon & Schuster. https://doi.org/10.1145/358916.361990

Ratna, N. N., Grafton, Q., & Macdonald, I. A. (2012). Does multiculturalism pay? Empirical evidence from the United States and Canada. *Economic Papers: A Journal of Applied Economics and Policy, 31*(4), 401–417. https://doi.org/10.1111/1759-3441.12003

Raymond Gann, R. (2004). Language, conflict and community: linguistic accommodation in the urban US. *Changing English, 11*(1), 105–114. https://doi.org/10.1080/1358684042000179471

Reich, H. H., & Krumm, H.J. (2013). *Sprachbildung und Mehrsprachigkeit: Ein Curriculum zur Wahrnehmung und Bewältigung sprachlicher Vielfalt im Unterricht.* Waxmann.

Ricento, T. (2014). Thinking about language: what political theorists need to know about language in the real world. *Language Policy, 13*(4), 351–369. https://doi.org/10.1007/s10993-014-9322-2

Riera-Gil, E. (2019). The communicative value of local languages: An underestimated interest in theories of linguistic justice. *Ethnicities, 19*(1), 174–199. https://doi.org/10.1177/1468796818786310

Robert, E. (2009). Accommodating "new" speakers? An attitudinal investigation of L2 speakers of Welsh in south-east Wales. *International Journal of the Sociology of Language, 195*, 93–115. https://doi.org/10.1515/IJSL.2009.007

Rollock, N., Gillborn, D., Vincent, C., & Ball, S. (2011). The public identities of the black middle classes: Managing race in public spaces. *Sociology, 45*(6), 1078–1093. https://doi.org/10.1177/0038038511416167

Rudmin, F. W. (2003). Critical history of the acculturation psychology of assimilation, separation, integration, and marginalization. *Review of General Psychology, 7*(1), 3–37. https://doi.org/10.1037%2F1089-2680.7.1.3

Ruiz, R. (2010). Reorienting language-as-resource. In J. E. Petrovic (Ed.), *International perspectives on bilingual education: Policy, practice, and controversy*, 155–172. Information Age Publishing.

Ryan, S. (2006). Language learning motivation within the context of globalization: An L2 self within an imagined global community. *Critical Inquiry in Language Studies*, *3*(1), 23–45. https://doi.org/10.1207/s15427595cils0301_2

Saldaña, J. (2015). *The coding manual for qualitative researchers*. Sage.

Sall, D. (2020). Selective acculturation among low-income second-generation West Africans. *Journal of Ethnic and Migration Studies*, *46*(11), 2199–2217. https://doi.org/10.1080/1369183X.2019.1610367

Sankoff, G. (2001). Linguistic outcomes of language contact. In P. Trudgill, J. Chambers & N. Schilling-Estes (Eds.), *Handbook of sociolinguistics*, 638–668. Basil Blackwell. https://doi.org/10.1002/9780470756591.ch25

Sarroub, L. K., & Quadros, S. (2014). Critical pedagogy in classroom discourse. In M. Bigelow, & J. Ennser-Kananen (Eds.), *The Routledge handbook of educational linguistics*. Routledge.

Schiefer, D., & van der Noll, J. (2017). The Essentials of social cohesion: A literature review. *Social Indicators Research*, *132*, 579–603. https://doi.org/10.1007/s11205-016-1314-5

Schieffelin, B., & Ochs, E. (Eds.). (1986). *Language socialization across cultures*. Cambridge University Press.

Schieffelin, B.B., Woolard, K.A., & Kroskrity, P.V. (Eds). (1998). Language ideologies: practice and theory. *Oxford studies in anthropological linguistics, 16*. Oxford University Press.

Schiffman, H. (1996). *Linguistic culture and language policy (The politics of language)*. Routledge. https://doi.org/10.4324/9780203021569

Seidlhofer, B. (2011). *Understanding English as a lingua franca*. Oxford University Press. https://doi.org/10.1111/j.1473-4192.2011.00305.x

Sengupta, P. (2018). Language as identity in colonial India. Palgrave Macmillan.

Shafie, L. A., Yaacob, A., & Paramjit Kaur, K. S. (2015). The roles of English language and imagined communities of a Facebook group. *International Journal of Emerging Technologies in Learning*, *10*(6), 21–26. https://doi.org/10.3991/ijet.v10i6.4831

Shi, X. (2011). Negotiating power and access to second language resources: A study on short-term Chinese MBA students in America. *Modern Language Journal*, *95*(4), 575–588. https://doi.org/10.1111/j.1540-4781.2011.01245.x

Shrestha, M., Wilson, S., & Singh, M. (2008). Knowledge networking: A dilemma in building social capital through nonformal education. *Adult Education Quarterly, 58*(2), 129–150. https://doi.org/10.1177/0741713607310149

Siddaway, A. (2014). What is a systematic literature review and how do I do one? *University of Stirling*, *1*, 1–13.

Skutnabb-Kangas, T. (1981). *Bilingualism or not: The education of minorities*. Multilingual Matters.

Smala, S., Bergaz Paz, J., & Lingard, B. (2013). Languages, cultural capital and school choice: distinction and second language immersion programs. *British*

Journal of Sociology of Education, *34*(3), 373–391. https://doi.org/10.1080/01425692.2012.722278

Smirnova, A., & Iliev, R. (2017). Political and linguistic identities in an ethnic conflict. *Journal of Language and Social Psychology*, *36*(2), 211–225. https://doi.org/10.1177/0261927X16643559

Stolle, K. (2013). Didaktik und Methodik im Bereich Deutsch als Fremdsprache. *Zeitschrift für Interkulturellen Fremdsprachenunterricht*, *18*(1), 146–164.

Straubhaar, R. (2013). Student use of aspirational and linguistic social capital in an urban immigrant-centered English immersion high school. *High School Journal*, *97*(2), 92–106. https://doi.org/10.1353/hsj.2013.0026

Studer, H. (2006). *Hochdeutsch im Kindergarten: Konzept zur systematischen Förderung des Hochdeutschen in den Kindergärten des Kantons Graubünden*. Pädagogische Hochschule Graubünden. www.gr.ch/DE/institutionen/verwaltung/ekud/avs/Volksschule/Standard_KG_Konzept_de.pdf

Sturges, K. M., Cramer, E. D., Harry, B., & Klingner, J. K. (2005). Desegregated but unequal: Some paradoxes of parent involvement at Bromden elementary. *International Journal of Educational Policy, Research, and Practice: Reconceptualizing Childhood Studies*, *6*(1), 79–104.

Tamura, E. H. (1993). The English-only effort, the anti-Japanese campaign, and language acquisition in the education of Japanese Americans in Hawaii, 1915–40. *History of Education Quarterly*, *33*(1), 37–58. https://doi.org/10.2307/368519

Taylor, S. E., Peplau, L. A., & Sears, D. O. (2006). *Social psychology* (International Ed.). Pearson.

Thomas, J., & Harding, A. (2008). Methods for the thematic synthesis of qualitative research in systematic reviews. *BMC Medical Research Methodology*, *8*(45). https://doi.org/10.1186/1471-2288-8-45

Todd, R.W., & Pojanapunya, P. (2009). Implicit attitudes towards native and non-native speaker teachers. *System 37*, 23–33. https://doi.org/10.1016/j.system.2008.08.002

Tollefson, J. (1991). *Planning language, planning inequality: Language policy in the community*. Longman.

Trice, A. G. (2004). Mixing it up: International graduate students' social interactions with American students. *Journal of College Student Development*, *45*(6), 671–687. https://doi.org/10.1353/csd.2004.0074

Trudgill, P. (1974). *The social differentiation of English in Norwich*. Cambridge University Press.

UNDP (2020). *Strengthening social cohesion: Conceptual framing and programming implications*. United Nations Development Programme.

United Nations (2015). Sustainable development: The 17 Goals. https://sdgs.un.org/goals

Valdez, V.E., Freire, J.A., & Delavan, M. (2016). The gentrification of dual language education. *The Urban Review*, *48*, 601–627. https://doi.org/10.1007/s11256-016-0370-0

Van Lange, P. A. M., Higgins, E. T., & Kruglanski, A. W. (Eds.). (2020). *Social psychology: Handbook of basic principles* (3rd ed.). The Guilford Press.

Vedder, P. H., Sam, D., & Liebkind, K. (2007). The acculturation and adaptation of Turkish adolescents in north-western Europe. *Applied Development Science, 11*(3), 126–136. https://doi.org/10.1080/10888690701454617

Vega, W., Ang, A., Rodriguez, M., & Finch, B. (2011). Neighborhood protective effects on depression in Latinos. *American Journal of Community Psychology, 47*(1), 114–126. https://doi.org/10.1007/s10464-010-9370-5

Vertovec, S. (2007). Super-diversity and its implications. *Ethnic and Racial Studies, 30*(6), 1024–1054. https://doi.org/10.1080/01419870701599465

Vetter, E. (2015). Re-thinking language conflict: challenges and options. *International Journal of the Sociology of Language, 235*, 103–118. doi 10.1515/ijsl-2015-0016

Watson-Gegeo, K. (2004). Mind, language, and epistemology: Toward a language socialization paradigm for SLA. *Modern Language Journal, 68*, 331–350. https://doi.org/10.1111/j.0026-7902.2004.00233.x

Wernicke, M., & Bournot-Trites, M. (2011). Introducing the CEFR in BC: Questions and challenges. *Canadian Journal of Applied Linguistics / Revue canadienne de linguistique appliquee, 14*(2), 106–128.

Wodak, R. (2007). Discourses in European Union organizations: Aspects of access, participation, and exclusion. *TEXT and TALK, 27*(5–6), 655–680. https://doi.org/10.1515/TEXT.2007.030

Wodak, R. (2012). Language, power and identity. *Language Teaching, 45*(2), 215–233. https://doi.org/10.1017/S0261444811000048

Woo, D., & Giles, H. (2017). Language attitudes and intergroup dynamics in multilingual organizations. *International Journal of Cross Cultural Management, 17*(1), 39–52. https://doi.org/10.1177%2F1470595817701507

Worley, C. (2005). 'It's not about race. It's about the community': New Labour and 'community cohesion'. *Critical Social Policy, 25*(4), 483–496. https://doi.org/10.1177%2F0261018305057026

Worthy, J., & Rodriguez-Galindo, A. (2006). "Mi hija vale dos personas": Latino immigrant parents' perspectives about their children's bilingualism. *Bilingual Research Journal, 30*(2), 579–601. https://doi.org/10.1080/15235882.2006.10162891

Wright, S. (2004). *Language policy and language planning: From nationalism to globalisation*. Palgrave Macmillan.

Wright, S. C., & Bougie, É. (2007). Intergroup contact and minority-language education: Reducing language-based discrimination and its negative impact. *Journal of Language and Social Psychology, 26*(2), 157–181. https://doi.org/10.1177/0261927X07300078

Yahya, S., Bekerman, Z., Sagy, S., & Boag, S. (2012). When education meets conflict: Palestinian and Jewish-Israeli parental attitudes towards peace promoting education. *Journal of Peace Education, 9*(3), 297–320. https://doi.org/10.1080/17400201.2012.698386

Yates, L. (2011). Interaction, language learning and social inclusion in early settlement. *International Journal of Bilingual Education and Bilingualism, 14*(4), 457–471. https://doi.org/10.1080/13670050.2011.573068

Yiakoumetti, A., & Mina, M. (2013). Language choices by teachers in EFL classrooms in Cyprus: Bidialectism meets bilingualism with a call for teacher training programmes in linguistic variation. *Teacher Development, 17*(2), 1–15. https://doi.org/10.1080/13664530.2012.753943

Appendix

Themes, sub-themes and descriptive codes

This appendix illustrates our coding structure (Table A.1) that was developed as described in Chapter 3. Many of the statements we identified in the articles were coded under more than one sub-theme. This means that articles can appear in more than one sub-theme. This explains why the number of articles coded at the sub-theme level does not add up with that indicated at the main theme level. In order to make transparent under what theme and sub-theme these articles were coded, the reader can access the EndNote Library (Meier, Smala & Lawson, 2021), which offers full references to the articles.

Table A.1 Themes, sub-themes and descriptive codes

Themes and sub-themes	Name of descriptive free codes	N of codes	N of articles per theme
Theme A:	**Potential social networks and access to resources through languages**		**181**
Social networks and resources	Languages enable access to resources	54	107
	Languages enable home-school ties	14	
	Languages enable intergenerational ties	9	
	Languages enable different types of networks	49	
	Languages enable strong ties	7	
Lack of social networks and resources	Limited home-school ties	2	29
	Limited intergenerational ties	3	
	Limited access to resources	10	
	Exclusive ties	15	

Table A.1 Cont.

Themes and sub-themes	Name of descriptive free codes	N of codes	N of articles per theme
Language competence as a resource	Dominant language	25	120
	Lack of dominant language	22	
	Loss of minority languages	4	
	Foreign languages	6	
	Multilingual competence	62	
	Other	10	
Theme B:	**Attitudinal/ideological dimension to languages and social cohesion**		**111**
Ideologically informed values and beliefs about languages	Monolingual orientations	37	111
	Multilingual orientations	31	
	Local vs translocal orientation	3	
	L perceived as problem	6	
	L as proxy for other problems	52	
	Addressing L not enough	5	
	Other	1	
Theme C:	**Languages and sense of belonging to social groups**		**104**
Belonging	Languages as markers of group identity	17	83
	to dominant groups	7	
	to imagined groups	19	
	to linguistic in-groups	14	
	to several linguistic groups	27	
Contested belonging	Difficulty to belong to group	13	21
	Resistance to belong	9	
Theme D:	**Bottom-up language decisions and behaviour (social action)**		**227**
Practices in education	Involving parents with diverse languages	57	87
	Language and language groups segregated	61	
	Validation of languages	60	
	Multilingual practices	62	
	Multilingual teachers	55	
Communication	Multilingual communication	20	73
	Shared majority languages	7	
	Shared minority languages	38	

Table A.1 Cont.

Themes and sub-themes	Name of descriptive free codes	N of codes	N of articles per theme
Language varieties	English as a dominant languages	24	66
	English as a lingua franca	12	
	Language varieties	30	
	Bilingual practices	1	
	Other	1	
Social integration/ participation	Languages for social integration/ participation	45	57
	Other social integration/participation	15	
Social segregation	Conflict between language groups	21	79
	Exclusion due to language	43	
	Language hampers integration	17	
	Language conflict addressed discursively	3	
	Other	3	
Theme E:	**Top-down language decisions (language policy and planning)**		**162**
Language policy	Encourage linguistic diversity	30	78
	Encourage monolingualism	36	
	Language minority under threat	14	
	Other	8	
Languages taught in education	Majority language	42	95
	Modern foreign languages	15	
	Mother tongues	30	
	Sign languages	2	
	Other	8	
Types of language education	Adult literacy education	7	52
	Bilingual education	39	
	Saturday schools	2	

Index